Wonderful
digital
Leadership

Christian Vandsø Andersen

Plazeebo Publishing

To my sons

Wonderful Digital Leadership
by Christian Vandsø Andersen
www.vandsoe.dk

Published by:
Plazeebo Publishing
www.plazeebo.com

ISBN 978-87-974121-0-7
1. edition 2022
Printed by KDP

Layout: ivimedia.dk
Illustrated by: Eva Ehler

Contents

Farming looks mighty easy when your plow is a pencil and you're a thousand miles from the corn field

Dwight D. Eisenhower

Wonderful is about being full of wonder

Wonderful:
/ˈwʌndəfʊlˌ'wʌndəf(ə)l/
Filled with wonder.
Inspiring delight

This is a book of wonder – a book about digital leadership. Wonderful leadership. Today, wonderful is an adjective we use to describe something positively. "What a wonderful dress." Etymologically, wonderful is an Old English combined word for "*filled with wonder.*" This book is filled with wonder, and the purpose of the book is to get you, the reader, to wonder.

Wonder why. Wonder how. Wonder who. The objective is for you to be wonder-full.

As you wonder and gain new insights, please share your wonderings with the world. Together, we make the world more knowledgeable as we continue to be curious and filled with wonder.

Foreword

Rushing into action, you fail.
Trying to grasp things, you lose them.
Forcing a project to completion,
you ruin what was almost ripe.

Therefore the Master takes action
by letting things take their course.
He remains as calm at the end
as at the beginning.
He has nothing,
thus has nothing to lose.
What he desires is non-desire;
what he learns is to unlearn.
He simply reminds people
of who they have always been.
He cares about nothing but the Tao.
Thus he can care for all things.

Lao Tzu, Tao Te Ching

Dear reader,

If you are looking for the latest best practice guide to leadership, then put this book back on the shelf. This book was written by someone who believes in magic, even though it cannot be explained, and realizes that quality requires that constraints be loosened to let it flow.

Christian's view of leadership is one where the focus is not on the leader, their decisions, and infinite wisdom, but on how they free people enough to do great work. The skills for this look less like MBAs (even though Christian has a couple) and more like old-fashioned trust and listening. These seem simple enough, but Christian has a gift of making them real, with the effect of seeing people. I know this because I have experienced it first-hand.

Christian and I met over a shared interest in complexity science. He, a senior executive at the LEGO group; I, a struggling entrepreneur responding to multiple problems while climbing the corporate ladder. By most standards of success, I was a failure, but Christian saw me as someone whose voice deserved to be heard, trying to change "the system."

Christian's work has taught me practical ways to think about emergence and timing. His flow description is the most down-to-earth yet accurate way to describe the creative process as I have experienced it. And because of his making explicit what I tacitly knew, I now respect when the time is right for me to write and crawl out of bed while words come to my mind in the early morning.

Do not be fooled by the simple, casual tone this book takes. Christian has the rare skill of taking some of the most theoretical materials and translating them into practical explanations. His deep respect for complexity helps him trust what he may not initially understand. He leans out when others would increase control, thus bringing awareness to the diversity of thought needed for quality.

Read this to understand how your humanity – a thing that you already have but maybe do not give yourself enough permission to use – can help you lead great teams.

Sarah Freiesleben
Digital Humanist

A book for leaders of digital teams

You have a manual for your car. You want to get the most out of this important and expensive asset, so even though you're not a mechanic or a race driver, you spend some time getting familiar with this asset. How does it work? What are some of the dos and don'ts of owning and driving a car?

This manual is for you if you are the boss (or the boss's boss) of software engineers or similar digital talent. It informs you how to optimize your outcomes, read the signals, and understand what they tell you. It shows you how to take care of your "asset," so it will serve you well for many years.

This book is mainly for leaders of people who craft digital solutions. The gap in the market that this book fills is simply that no one, to my knowledge, has ever written a manual on how to lead a digital team – with a focus on software engineers – as *they* would like to be led. Some have made assumptions, but if you haven't crafted software yourself, it's hard to understand what makes software developers tick.

It is especially for those of you that haven't been "in the trenches" for a while, or indeed if you've never been a software developer in your life, but due to the curveballs life has thrown at you, you find yourself as the boss of an organization that employs software engineers.

The book is structured such that, in the end, everything hopefully makes sense. To be true to the purpose of getting the reader to wonder, some chapters might at first read seem out of place to interrupt the readers' chain of thought.

You might benefit from reading the summary chapter at the end to build an internal scaffold of the wonderful journey we are about to embark on together.

Digital teams work in kairos, not chronological time

Wonder why the detailed plan has become "currency" in big companies? Even with companies that subscribe to agile ways of working, where responding to change is more important than following a plan. Yet we still see these bold, detailed plans showing exactly how we can reach a perfect future. The culprit is us – humans. We are all hedonistic to a degree, and when our brain sees this ideal future, it releases dopamine as a reward because looking at a goal is like realizing it. As we imagine the goal, our brain instantly reduces our engagement because we already got part of the reward. So – even if the world wasn't complex and we could make detailed plans, it is still counterproductive. Project managers will try to force you to deliver on plan – not because they are evil, but because they are humans.

For many years we have been trained to create chronological plans. We develop visions named by a year. We make business plans in quarters. We create delivery plans by date. We plan our day in time slots. The more straightforward the task, the more convenient it is to use time as the X-axis of a plan. But challenges arise when complexity sneaks in and disrupts the X-axis. Is there a better alternative to the traditional plan? Does an X-axis exist that can survive disruptions?

One of the biggest disruptors in the modern business world is probably the corona virus. Seemingly out of the blue, we changed our way of working and living. Some businesses faced huge losses – especially theaters, concerts, and retail – while other companies blossomed, such as e-commerce, take-away, and hand sanitizers.

None of these businesses had in their roadmap *"... and then a global pandemic happens in year 3 of our 5-year business plan"*. Obviously, no one could have predicted that. Yet, most roadmaps and business plans are executed by looking at the current world status and creating a desirable future scenario. We have become so accustomed to the idea of the x-axis of any plan to be the chronological time that we have difficulty even fathoming an alternative.

But there is an alternative. It's called καιρός.

In ancient Greece, they had two words for time. The Greeks used "chronos" to depict our etymologically inherited

The ancient Greeks used the word "kairos" to depict a sense of time that was qualitative in nature.

concept of linear time; hours, days, weeks, months, and years passing "chronologically" as we move toward the future.

But they also used the word "kairos" to depict a sense of time that was qualitative in nature.

An example of a kairos time is the time when it's right to propose to your partner. It's not opportune to think, "I will propose at 11:47 next Wednesday". Most people that have proposed have been carrying the ring in a pocket, waiting for the right time.

If you have ever shot a bow or a rifle, when is the right time to release the bowstring or pull the trigger? It's a feeling—a knack. A time, not in chronos but in kairos. The examples of moments in kairos, not chronos are countless. Ask a fighter when the right time is to give a devastating right hook to the opponent in the ring. Ask a couple on a date when is the right time to attempt that first kiss. Ask a soldier when it's time to shoot the rifle.

We can extract this concept and insert it into a business context. What if a product launch wasn't planned for chronos time but in kairos? How would that look? How would we work if we tuned ourselves more to sense the emergence of the right time instead of a pre-determined, often arbitrarily, selected chronological time? Can we replace "now is the time" with "when the time is right?"

When working on a product or an outcome that has external

It's time when the conditions are right, completely detached from the time on a watch. So detached, that the ancient Greeks found it advantageous to use two different words, because the difference between "the right time" and "the right time" was simply too grand.

dependencies, it often makes sense to keep deadlines in chronos.

If you invite people to a party, it is practical if they show up at the same time. Ideally, you would plan a party in kairos time. What if it is an event that takes place outside? Then you would prefer to throw the party on a warm and sunny day. You don't know if it is raining on the date where you planned it. But, to assemble the guests, we accept that risk and set a chronos date. However, we don't know if that day is the perfect day. Some might have a headache. Some would rather watch the big game. But alas, we depend on people showing up together, so we accept that risk. So don't throw away all your hard-earned Prince 2 project management skills – there are some exceptions where a deadline in chronos is necessary.

However, most of the deadlines we face are artificial or even arbitrary. They are created in chronos time because that is how we are used to planning. Especially when cooperating with other individuals, we take the easy way and set deadlines. Deadlines that are created in a meeting room. Deadlines that are the best guess by a group of people when it is opportune to launch a product or service. Deadlines are the easy choice when operating with internal or external stakeholders because they make reporting easy. It's easy to see if a deadline is met or to insist on it being fulfilled. Easy, as in it does not require more work than to look at the calendar and see if the product has launched. Our hedonistic brain loves easy things. The alternative is that we need to probe.

Get data. We need to make sense of this data. "Is now the right time?" And then we need to respond.

When the Corona pandemic made its unexpected entry, some businesses stuck to their guns whilst others reacted swiftly and saw this as an opportunity. Two local escape rooms come to mind. I could probably invent an example closer to the theory. Still, I like this one because it actually happened and describes the difference between following a chronos roadmap and a kairos roadmap. Note that there is more to it than just roadmaps, though. The first one saw customers stray away from escape rooms. They planned to upgrade the puzzles and introduce new rooms to gain market share. Their advisors told them to pack up all the puzzles and store them in a cheap storage locker. They would not renew their lease on the property where they had previously held escape room sessions, nor would they renew the contracts for the hourly paid staff. When the corona epidemic was over, they pulled the puzzles out of the storage locker, rented a new property, and hired new staff, ready to continue their plan. They had lost income for a couple of years but minimized the loss as much as possible.

The other escape room, which happened to reside just a few blocks away, saw the Corona epidemic as an opportunity. Now was the opportune time to try something new. They bought a GoPro camera[1] for each staff member and set up a

---

1. A small versatile camera you can strap to your chest or forehead

simple streaming service on their website. Now customers could try out the escape room from their homes. Everyone could see the stream from the GoPro cameras and from each other, provided they had a webcam or were using a tablet with a camera. The escape room saw a boom in customers – not just from their existing customer base but also from new customers, such as companies with employees in different countries – all of whom were now able to do virtual team-building sessions. They also could use puzzles that had previously been deemed unsuitable because they were too fragile and couldn't stand up to the wear and tear of the guests. And they could even do much more advanced rooms because they could control the viewpoints. When the restrictions were lifted, they now had two businesses –a virtual escape room and a physical one.

Both escape rooms probably desired the same outcome – to be the most profitable in the area. But the first was firmly stuck in chronos time, and the only solution to survive a pandemic was to pause the progression on the roadmap. Pause, and hibernate as cheaply as possible until standard operating procedures can recommence. The other was living in kairos time, maybe even using kairos roadmaps.

A kairos roadmap gives compass directions and not GPS routes. Instead of "drive 4 minutes, then turn left on Dunkirk Avenue," it would read "travel north until you see the lighthouse, then travel west, and beware of the sirens." A kairos roadmap is like a chart for the old sea travelers. It gives a direction, marks the possible dangers and risks, such

as low tides and tempting sirens, and marks opportunities, such as fertile lands or places where trading is optimal.
The time it would take to reach the destination would depend on wind, current, the occasional mutiny, pirates, etc.
Traveling by sea would always involve many external dangers, but a kairos-based roadmap is still valid, even after
unforeseen events.

Navigating a sailboat in uncharted waters is not unlike running a business. There will be challenges and opportunities.
Sometimes, there will be a headwind, sometimes a tailwind.
A rigid roadmap in chronos will soon become obsolete, while
a kairos roadmap that gives an overall direction and maps
out the risks and opportunities will retain its value. As mentioned, there's more to it than the roadmaps. The mindset

of having agency and acknowledging emergence are two of the things we will unpack later.

Let's look at an example: If we face an unexpected danger – a rabid dog suddenly appears, barking with a foaming mouth – we only need a small **probe** to **sense** that this means trouble, and we can **respond**. In a large organization, the act of probing, sensing, and responding is distributed, so even if facing an equal danger, an organization will react slower than a person. The risk might not be a single threat but the combination of various signals sensed by multiple people. Chances are, the danger your organization is facing is the same as your competitors. The winner is the one who completes the probe, sense, respond the fastest, and understands what is emerging.

Note that although you will see words and discourse from complexity throughout this book, it is not a book on complexity theory. Many books exist on that subject, and the world does not need another one. Please refer to work by, for example, David Snowden and his Cynefin framework for a great complexity framework. The Cynefin framework is detailed, nuanced, and excellent as a sense-making tool.

The first step in moving to a kairos mindset is acknowledging emergence. Like neurons creating consciousness or traders creating a stock market, small interacting objects form a system with qualities different from the objects themselves.

An example of an emergent system is the weather. Weather is complex and cannot be broken down to the sum of its parts. This might be why kairos as a word has survived in the Greek language. It is no longer a concept of time that differs from chronological time. Today, in Greek, the word kairos simply means "weather." The weather works in cycles. Weather emerges as the result of many small systems, unaware of their collective influence. Weather exists in kairos, and today, it is kairos.

Asking a digital team for an estimate of *"when is my product ready"* is like asking *"how long does it take to catch a fish"* or *"how long does it take to find a significant other."*

Working with digital products is complex. Market conditions change. Technology is changing. The users and their behavior are impossible to predict. Even the best planned digital product will receive positive and negative feedback when it launches, and the actual development of the product doesn't begin until the product is live, getting live feedback from users.

That doesn't mean deadlines are bad. A deadline can be an enabling constraint, and as we've seen, some things happen in chronos that requires just that. Especially when working with physical product launches, you often need chronos deadlines.

However, that does not mean the entire digital roadmap should be in chronos. As long as the scope is "create the most valuable product by this date, " kairos and chronos can easily go hand in hand.

"So – how do I ask the team for an estimate if they don't work in chronos?". The answer is: "you don't ask for estimates." What is the value of an estimate other than to control? Usually, a digital team is asked for an estimate because the manager/stakeholder/whoever is afraid they are spending a lot of money without getting anything in return. Hence, the most soothing thing to ask is, "*when* is the product done." The right thing to do is to work in small feedback loops with frequent deliveries and constantly work on the most valuable matter—delivering early and often. As the product matures with regular updates, the status and the speed of progress can be clearly demonstrated, and feedback can be incorporated with minimum disruption. This way of working, known by many names such as extreme programming (XP), Agile, and so forth, deserves a chapter on its own. We will take a meta-level look at agility in the next chapter.

Working in an agile team

Working in short feedback loops is something for which we already have methods, frameworks, and theories. Known by many names, under the umbrella of "agile," the idea of working in small learning loops, doing double loops every so often, fits nicely here.

Many great definitions of agile have been proposed, and many frameworks have been drawn. This is *a* definition (versus *the* definition) of agile for us to have a shared language. This definition is as right as it is wrong and only serves the purpose of creating a shared language.

The core of agile is the team. A cross-functional team fully empowered to reach a business goal in a psychologically safe environment.

There are artifacts and tools that the team can choose to use – *sprints*, *product owners*, *backlogs*, *retrospectives*, and so forth, but that is not part of agility, and you can have an agile team that uses none of those artifacts.

The empowerment gives discretion to the team to change the direction if need be. The team can change its methodology. They can change tools. They can even switch roles. The role needed in a sprint is like a menu card; the team decides who will take on which function in each sprint.

Fully functional means that the team has all the capabilities required to build the product within the group, meaning there are no handovers. No handovers from people designing to people building, to people testing. It's all teamwork, leading to less need for coordination and coordinators and higher throughput and efficiencies. In agile, the manager does not assign people to tasks; they give business outcomes to teams. Teams that work together produce output by team-work. We are so used to hearing "teamwork" that the word itself doesn't raise eyebrows. In other words, teamwork is a safe-to-say word that people will rarely question. If your organization truly believes in teamwork, other words shouldn't be there. "Accountability," "one throat to cho-ke." The idea of having a team accountable is quite strange to us. We tend to put someone in charge.

"If there's one person in charge, we know that that person has skin in the game, and we can always fire the person if the project fails to meet the deliverables. This gives us a very dedicated cap-tain that will ensure project success!"

At first read, this sentence seems to be quite fair. But scratching a bit on the surface, this mindset is dangerous for any agile team.

When was the last time you heard the word "accountability" used positively? When discussing projects, there is a hidden presupposition in "accountability if the project fails" and never "accountable if the project succeeds." Coincidentally, this also hinders psychological safety and trust.

What is trust? Is it a mathematical probability in believing that a person will behave in a certain way, or is it a com-plex neural process uniting diverse cognitive representati-ons? In either definition, trust (or lack thereof) will reflect in behaviors. As we build trust and psychological safety, the question arises if there is an upper limit to trust in the classical hierarchical structure of modern company structures. Can self-organizing, empowered teams build a higher degree of trust if the outcomes became teams' outcomes instead of the "one throat to choke" or "one neck to ring" philosophy where team outcomes are attributed to a single person? The team needs to be accountable for the product, not a person. Our hedonistic nature once again betrays us because it is easy to keep one person responsible. It is easy to enforce a penalty on one person, and it shows leadership to fire the project manager immediately after the project's failure.

Agile is particularly good when you don't know precisely how to achieve your outcome. You might need to change direction several times. The team works in short feedback loops, often called sprints, where experimentation and learning are essential. Since the team is working on something that hasn't been done before, there is no 'best practice'; hence learning and experimentation is imperative. The team needs to constantly learn, overcome, and adapt, and use those lessons learned to bring the product closer to achieving the business outcome.

Usually, the duration of a sprint is the shortest amount of time in which you can validate a hypothesis. Working in fixed chronological sprints is commonplace but not the most optimal way. It is a review cadence, not a delivery cadence. Agile teams work best in uncertain environments - sometimes known by the VUCA acronym. Volatile, Uncertain, Complex, and Ambiguous. You can't explain what you want in a single line item in such an environment. It would be best if you told a story about the user behavior, which the team then translates into one or more hypotheses on the required features. These stories are often called User Stories, originating from extreme programming, and it's an excellent litmus test to see if agile is for you. If you can describe what you want in a single line, you don't need agility, and a waterfall process might be better. Agile might be for you if you need to tell a story. Remember that a user story is always a "user" story. It must be told in the language and perspective of a user.

In agile, you try to 'always be finished,' not unlike a croquis drawing. If you've seen someone draw croquis, you'll know that it's always done – you use iterations to make it more complete. We can call it a 'walking skeleton' or 'vertical slice.' That is also how you get the status of a product. You see the current state when the team demonstrates the current

phase at the end of each sprint. You can follow the product as it matures and come with early input directly based on experience instead of a traffic light.

Given that you have a fixed team, your cost is the price of keeping that team alive and thus entirely predictable. If the team provides good value, you can continue to fund them or even increase the number of teams to minimize Cost-of-Delay. If the team does not create good value, you can stop the work and have the team work on something else— either something known to be valuable or to innovate and discover something new and useful.

What about agile frameworks?

Frameworks are appealing. Like the Sirens in Greek mytho-logy, they sing alluring songs telling of a better place by promising to tackle complexity with processes. But are agile frameworks just snake oil and an excuse to sell consultancy hours, or do they have merit?

Before we dive into an answer, let's take a route to a diffe-rent domain, namely Martial Arts.

There are a lot of different martial arts, and they build on different philosophies and occupy different, sometimes con-tradicting, modus operandi. Most of them have a progres-sion system in the form of belts, with the black belt being the most precious. The black belt, in many forms, is con-sidered the beginning of the journey, not the end. In Ka-rate, the Japanese word for black belt literally means "first step" – *sho dan*. The black belt is not the end goal. Instead, you have now learned the basics well enough to explore and

learn the art. Look at a well-worn black belt – it is a white belt underneath, and the more wear and tear the black belt is exposed to, the whiter it becomes. The more you learn, the more you understand what it is that you don't know. This focus on learning is something we can bring into our digital world.

Asking *"Which agile framework is the best"* is like asking *"Which form of martial art is the best."* Maybe it is the style of Bruce Lee? In the 1960s, Bruce Lee coined *Jeet Kune Do*. Bruce Lee was known as a hot head and often got into fights, but realized that sticking to his origins (Wing Chun) didn't hold up in a real fight. Jeet Kune Do was invented as a martial art without form, and it was one of the origins of what is today known as "mixed martial arts" or simply MMA. In the 1990s, MMA as a fighting contest became institutionalized and televised. The premise was simple: Two fighters entered a contained space – often an octagon – and were allowed to use the most appropriate fighting style to outclass the other.

Finally, we would learn which technique was the best. The winners of MMA fights will all be using the same martial arts style, right? The best martial art style would surely prevail.

When a fight starts, the fighter probes, senses, and responds. What is the other person doing? When? How? Why? You will see the probe clearly if you watch almost any MMA fight. The fighters extend their hands as if trying to touch an imaginary point where their fists would meet. They are throwing feints – not to inflict damage but to see and understand the reaction pattern. The probing is something that goes across many different styles. In Wing Chun there's the *"man sao,"* which means *"the asking hand."* In Muay Thai you'll see *"the touching hand,"* and in other styles, it's called "monitoring" or "checking." It's the first sequence in a probe-sense-respond cycle as we know it from complexity theory. So – who will win? Is it the style with the best probe or the best response?

As it turns out, it is the most skilled and well-trained fighter that wins, and very few of these winners use just one single form. Usually, an MMA fight begins with striking and kicking, using methods from karate and boxing, and ends up in a grappling match on the floor, using wrestling and jiu-jitsu. As it turns out, relying on the patterns of a single martial art doesn't allow you to win unless the opponent is also limited to that same art. When push comes to shove, we need to break the rules.

Now let's return to agile frameworks. Should you follow a theoretical framework?

If all projects behaved exactly like they do in theory, there wouldn't be a problem. But, in theory, there is no difference between theory and practice. And in practice, there's a vast difference between theory and practice.

There's an old Japanese saying called "Shu-ha-ri," which translates to: "First you learn the rules. Then you follow the rules. Then you break the rules". This saying has found its way into martial arts, game theory, and Lean. While the origins of the term remain uncertain, the concept is still strong. The literal translation of the kanji (the logographic Chinese characters used in writing Japanese) is actually 'Protect,' 'Detach,' and 'Transcend.' That became: Learn the rules, follow them, then break them and make them your own. Or – learn the framework, use the framework, and then make your own.

The problems with these frameworks are not the frameworks per se. It is the way they are introduced into the organization. Agile is like democracy or love. It can't be forced, and

Agile is like democracy or love. It can't be forced, and it can't be bought

it can't be bought. Sure, you can buy something that looks very much like love, but it's not the real thing.

Would you think it makes sense to talk about a relationship's 'end state'? Would you believe it if someone handed you a framework saying that 'this is the best practice of a relationship' and follow that framework? The answer is usually "of course not," and the reasons are that there are humans involved here and that no two relationships are the same. What works for one couple might not work for another. Then how is it that we believe corporations or projects are different? Are they not also comprised of people? Do they not differ from project to project? How is it that we think we can apply any sort of best practice in this arena but not another?

There's a hidden gem in the martial arts world that can also apply here. Back in the day, people transferred knowledge in different ways from today. They made stories into songs to make them easier to remember. Martial arts were transformed into a sequence to make them easier to remember. In karate, they are called Kata, and in Tae-Kwon-Do, they are called pumsae. The commonality is that it is a systematic, pre-arranged set of martial arts techniques. They are usually ordered from easy to difficult, so they have also made it into the belt grading system. Now a kata or pumsae are excellent memory scaffolds, but they are not useful for anything in and of themselves. You can't learn self-defense by just learning these moves. Instead, they need to be reverse engineered or broken down. The technique in karate is called Bun Kai – *to break down.* The purpose of these exercises is to look at the framework and figure out the original intent. What is the purpose of this move? If it's a block, what type of attack does it block? And then practice that in a real-life sparring session. How might you apply this to the myriad of agile frameworks? Could this be a method to determine if there might be valuable knowledge to glean from them?

Most of the modern agile frameworks were made in the same way. Someone observed something they liked or had some evidence that it worked, and collected that into a framework. Just like in martial arts, the framework might have been altered further – forgetting the original intent but making it easier to remember or 'sell' to the rest of the world. If you are unfortunate enough to find yourself in an organization practicing a framework by the letter, you should think about two things. Shuhari and Bunkai. Break down the framework, figure out the purpose, then break the rules and make something that works for you. Or, in the words of Bruce Lee[1]: *"Absorb what is useful, reject what is useless, add what is essentially your own."*

Organizing autonomous digital teams

A self-organizing, autonomous team is not a new term or concept. It is, for instance, present in an excerpt written in 1951 by Eric Trist and Ken Bamforth[2]. The article shows that working in smaller teams in the coal mines created more productivity and higher job satisfaction. The autonomous groups would work on what was most important right now, and if one team finished, they would go on and help another section – even if it was outside their field of experience. That helped to establish a broad understanding of the problems and made the teams understand the value they created even better. As the teams learn not only their own practice but also the practices of the teams they help, they essentially become learning systems, expanding their decision space and the ability to absorb and solve a variety of problems within the group. Trist and Bamforth coined the term "sociotechnical systems" as the interrelatedness of social and technical aspects of an organization.

If we take a bird's eye view of any organization, there are apparent groups of work/people/processes that belong together. To find these groups, start by imagining if you dropped the entire organization on the floor; where would the natural fracture planes be? There might be a group that deals with people. We can call this group HR. We would also identify other groups such as Marketing, Shipping, Sales, etc. If we do an ethnographic study on each of these groups (sometimes called *domains*) we will most likely identify some common traits of the domains and some immediate differences. One of these might be discourse. What does a word mean in each domain? In shipping, a "product" is perhaps described as having a weight, a height, a width, and an accompanying shipping cost. In Marketing, a "product" might be described as something with a "value proposition," "target demography," a "price point," and so on. The point is that they each have their own ubiquitous language – a term coined by Eric Evans in Domain Driven Design[3] (DDD). One of the advantages of looking at the organization as Domains and insisting on a ubiquitous language is that it makes communication easier between "the business" and the digital team. Another more technical advantage relates to software engineers' code. If there is an agreement on the ubiquitous language, it makes it easier to read and understand the code of others. The consistent and easy to understand language will increase collaboration and flow.

Let's explore the following hypothesis: Thinking about your organization as a collection of domains can enable a healthy architecture and efficient digital teams. This is also known as sociotechnical architecture.

It is not about scaling agile; it is about descaling work to fit an agile team.

As we discussed in the chapter on agility, the core of agile is small, self-organizing teams empowered to solve a business problem or opportunity. We often see organizations struggle with how to scale agile, and while there are several frameworks out there promising to do just that, it is probably not what the company wants.

It is not about scaling agile but about descaling work to fit an agile team. And that descaling can be done through sociotechnical systems such as domains.

Let's say you run a small business that sells products online. By mapping the teams into domains, you could choose to let your organization reflect in the domains. In 1967, the software engineer Melvin Conway coined what is now known as Conway's law. He initially said: "Any organization that designs a system (defined broadly) will produce a design whose structure is a copy of the organization's communication structure." Today, Conway's law is widely used to mean that the organization's output reflects the organizational structure. By organizing in domains, we are effectively doing what could be called an "inverse Conway." If the organization plays such a crucial role in the final product, then let's use that to our advantage accordingly.

Thus, a digital organization is not something that should be taken lightly. The organization is architecture, and it must be carefully devised. The definition of the domains must be constructed carefully, identifying the bounded contexts in which each domain resides. Within each domain, the teams must be full-featured to maximize flow and minimize bottlenecks. Each domain must have all the capabilities needed to produce the outcome for which they are accountable. The consequence is that the old matrix organization will not work at the top level. The top level of the organization must be domains, not capabilities like a matrix organization.

How you organize the next level - the subdomain level - is a matter of taste. You can organize the product teams directly as an organizational unit with a mix of capabilities, or you can choose to have a matrix and then have the leaders of these capability units be responsible for capability building. If your products are stable, option 1 is excellent, but it can be a counter-productive way of organizing if they are not. It is more difficult to dismantle a team if it is an organizational unit, and the team's sense of self-preservation might delay the right decision. Employees hate re-organizations. They hate to change managers and colleagues, so organizing in products will make it more difficult to dismantle products than if it were a matrix organization. There is a third option as well – we will touch on this when we introduce the concept of 'wicked problems' later.

There are several ways of identifying and describing domains. Domain Driven Design (DDD), being the first, is worth looking into, and Event Storming especially is a great process that can help you on the way. But if you work in a highly innovative environment, DDD might not be your only choice, as there is no optimal notion for "an emerging domain." A yet-to-be-defined domain that might become useful, pending user research and experimentation.

The roads to success are always different

"Necessity is the mother of invention." This phrase is found in different variations across cultures and timelines. Often, great inventions emerge from an immediate need. The system simply needs to reinvent itself to survive. One of the inventions from such a need was The Toyota Production System created in Japan – later renamed *Lean* by the west[4].

The success of Lean and the influence of Lean on digital and agility is evident. The efficiency of the Toyota Way is well documented and will not be repeated here. Instead, we will talk about what happens when you *copy* success instead of *learning* from success.

General Motors (GM) was the largest automaker and reigned supreme in the US market for many years (ironically, it was dethroned by none other than Toyota). They had a manufacturing plant called Fremont Assembly in Fremont, California, that was performing poorly. GM turned to Toyota, and together they formed *New United Motor Manufacturing Inc.* (NUMMI). The idea was simple – just copy the way they did it in Japan, and success would surely follow. So, they did. They were keeping the same people but copying the Toyota Way entirely. While this bold experiment should be applauded for bringing learning into this world, the NUMMI plan failed utterly. Employee satisfaction was at an all-time low, and productivity was horrible. NUMMI closed, and the majority of the plant is now owned by another car manufacturer that might sound familiar – Tesla. The Tesla plant is currently healthy and functioning, removing any traces of the failure of NUMMI (geographical placement, buildings, infrastructure, etc.)

The point of telling this story is to argue that digital teams are often presented with "evidence" that a given model or framework is good simply because someone else had success with it.

Some books boldly assert that "the successful companies used this methodology." What the books don't tell us is that there are just as many (if not more) unsuccessful companies using the same methodologies. It is not simply the methods that make us successful.

There is no silver bullet, no guaranteed operating model. The organization must be a learning organization to succeed.

Dampen the things that don't work, increase the ones that do. Run parallel, safe to fail probes all the time, listen for the weak signals the organization is feeding back and try to create positive inference

Dampen the things that don't work and increase the ones that do. Run parallel, safe-to-fail probes, listen for the weak signals the organization is feeding back, and try to create favorable interference. Unless your company is producing a commodity with no differentiators, it is a unique company in every way. The culture, the customers, the values – the entire rationale for the company's right to have a market share footprint – is unique to this company.

Of course, learning from successful people and companies is to be encouraged. Learn from the mistakes and the successes. Copying successful processes without learning and understanding is called "Cargo Cult". Cargo Cult refers to the indigenous behavior of Melanesian tribes in the aftermath of World War II. During the war, planes would land on the islands where the tribes lived. As a token of appreciation for using their land, the aircraft usually left food, gear, or other valuable things to the tribes. That ensured the planes could continue using the islands as a base during the war, and the tribes were happy to receive the loot. However, the war ended, and the planes stopped arriving, much to the frustration of the tribes on the islands. The tribes tried to copy all the actions leading to a plane landing. They built bamboo control towers. They lit up a landing strip with torches and had a man waving bamboo sticks on the runway. They made a hut and had a man sitting there with two half coconuts on each ear, talking into a stick. This is Cargo Cult – all the right actions but none of the expected results. Cargo Cult happens when one company copies what another company has done without understanding the deeper rationale. Cargo Cult lives on well today in 'best practice,' agile methods, and made-for-purpose words like Digital Disruption.

Naturally, we need a word for something before we start talking about it, and with terms come institutions.

For instance, a phrase like "mental illness." Before those words were coined, people were "lunatics" - which literally means "moon sick" - or the word used was simply "madness." But after the term "mental illness" came into common parlance, we found ourselves with mental institutions and diagnoses. We could help many more people because now we could differentiate between different types of mental illnesses.

Disruption is not a positive word. Ruption stems from Latin "*ruptura,*" meaning rupture or breaking (like breaking a leg). It is the same ruption found in cor*ruption* and bank*ruptcy*. We are told that disruption is when something new comes into a well-established structure and completely changes it and that we need to think differently about disruption.

Disruption has been around since the dawn of time. When we domesticated animals, invented weapons, or created fire, we disrupted society. We disrupted the market by developing the wheel, the plow, and the steam engine. When back loading and breech-loading rifles met muzzle-loading rifles, the game of war was disrupted. When sub-prime loans were introduced, the financial market was disrupted. Both the word and the action are neither new nor newsworthy, and the current discourse is better off without them. For a word to effect change, it needs to enable something that wasn't there before. The thing with "disruption" is that it has become an elaborate excuse. It has been presented as something new, and because of this, no one could have seen it coming. A lot of people, therefore, are now creating presentations on how to prepare for digital disruption. We see companies publicly saying they are on a digital disruption journey, which sounds like a good idea for all intents and purposes. While digital certainly has the power to make a lot of things easier or more fun, it is still just a tool. It's a means rather than an end, but it gets lost in complication. Let's say you run a customer service department suffering too long waiting times, and your company has bought into the paradigm of digital disruption. You would immediately start to seek out digital tools to solve the waiting time. You invested in chatbots and autogenerated answering pages, and everybody is happy. However, the right approach would be to look at the entire company and determine the root cause. Maybe there's a problem in the supply chain, and a particular piece of your product is always malfunctioning, causing people to call customer service. Or there is a new intern in marketing making incorrect claims on your YouTube channel, saying your product can do X instead of Y, causing people to call customer service. Making it a mission to achieve "digital disruption" is a fallacy, and as we have just seen, disruption has been part of life on Earth since long before humankind, and calling it something else is just that - an excuse. Instead, be specific about what your organization wants to do. Try to avoid buzzwords and instead tell a captivating story.

A typical day for a software engineer

Stereotypes are everywhere, leading to cognitive bias, an unintended behavior. Consider a software engineer as an exaggerated bias: It's a male. He has glasses as thick as the bottom of cola bottles, of which he consumes a lot. He is not in great physical shape; he is ungainly in his people's skills, and his hygiene leaves a lot to be desired. Or maybe she's a woman; she does Crossfit and has excellent people skills. Today, digital talents come in any shape and form, and your first mistake would be to look at them as engineers first and people second. When you meet an engineer, try to hold back your bias and see the person. When you recruit an engineer, remember that you are recruiting a person. When you organize your team or teams, remember first and foremost that they are made up of people. People with personalities are not the same as people with skills. The team might look robust from a capability point of view, but team spirit and collaboration are just as important. A skilled team that cannot collaborate will never produce a great product.

Sometimes, the team constellation is just too uniform, causing friction as team members fight over the same work. Or, the team constellation is too diverse, leaving no one for functional sparring.

Many of the books you have read on leadership apply equally here as well – software engineers are no different from any other human being. Or rather, they ARE JUST AS different. But what they do is something special.

It's an art. It's a craft. It's a science. And here's what you need to know.

Let's begin with a typical day for a software engineer.

It is essential to know that "a day" in this context is equivalent to a typical working day, but given that software engineering is just as much an art as it is a science, inspiration and motivation must be present before good code can be written. It is impossible to schedule when a software engineer will write good code. Given that most work in teams, when that happens has been more conformed in recent times, but some still write their best code in the middle of the night. Granted, if the job is simple, any adequate engineer can code it at any time of the day. But if it's a big, hairy audacious problem, the muse just has to be there. Software development is never a 9-to-5 job. If the code to be written is complex, it requires the software engineer to be "in the zone." It takes effort, time, and energy to get into the zone, and once "in there," it's disruptive to be disturbed. Thus, you will see engineers meeting up for work, doing apparent non-working-related things before attending the daily stand-up, kicking off the day. Not because the person is lazy; they're just warming up to get into the zone.

Some use the daily stand-up to get an overview of what to do today. What are the impediments, what are the dependencies, and so on? Others have tools that will give them the same info, and while many teams start the day with a stand-up meeting and a coffee, it is perfectly fine if the team has chosen not to.

Let's follow "Joe" around. Joe is a software engineer by heart, trade, and craft.

When Joe has a rough idea of what work to do, the latest code version is fetched from the versioning system. Joe is happy to see that his development environment is identical to the production environment. It has the same libraries, the same servers, and the same naming. He makes a minor change to the code and commits the code. "Commit" is developer lingo for putting the code in the versioning system. Joe smiles when the pipeline works as intended, and all the unit tests are green except one. Joe quickly looks at it, finds a bug, and patches it. Afterward, everything is green. Joe takes a minute to ponder.

Way back when, code was stored on punch cards or punch tape and introduced the words "bug" and "patch." An actual bug could cause a punch tape to fail, and to fix your code; you would literally cut out the faulty code with a bug on it and patch in a new, fixed piece of tape. The work was divided between those writing and those implementing the code by punching holes. Today, this work is consolidated into the same capability. But another division of labor existed in software engineering. For a long time, someone was writing code, and someone else would deploy it, run it, and monitor it. Software engineering was divided into "development" and "operations." Today, we know that it makes little sense. If you write your code, you own it and operate it. After all, who knows better how to operate your code than you, and it does mean you give a little extra attention to your deployment if you know that it's your phone that rings if the application breaks. This is why Joe likes CI/CD. CI stands for "Continuous Integration" and is a way of automatically building and testing Joe's code with the rest of the code base – the trunk – to ensure he hasn't inadvertently broken something somewhere else. The CD pipeline makes sure to deploy the code to production (in some cases, it just packages the code and makes it ready for deployment). Therefore, you sometimes hear that CD means "Continuous Delivery" and sometimes "Continuous deployment." Joe would expect that the company has one or more modern and solid CI/CD pipeline(s) ready for him to use. It is often not something he wants to spend a lot of time on. Once the code is written and works, it should be easy to put into production. The idea of developing and operating your product is sometimes called DevOps, although that term has been overloaded to mean more than just removing the dichotomy between development and operations.

Joe cracks his knuckles, puts his noise-canceling headset on, and fires up his favorite IDE. An IDE stands for Integrated Development Environment, which is basically an editor, a debugger, and some local build automation. Joe uses the same IDE as everyone else in his team, making it easier to help each other because the other teammates immediately recognize the layout. He is not forced to use it, and sometimes he fires up his trusty old Emacs, but he knows it makes sense to stick to the team's choice.

The keyboard starts clicking. Joe likes a mechanical keyboard. He knows that Denise next to him is a sucker for low-travel membrane keyboards. Since most of his work must travel through his fingers, he can have an opinion on which keyboard to use. Something people primarily working in PowerPoint and email will never understand. This thought makes Joe smile, and he chuckles lightly, which no one hears because his teammates are all in the zone.

Do not disturb a software engineer that looks to be in the zone. Engineers can multitask but being in the zone is sacred. It is similar to being asleep. You can wake me up, but it will take me some time to go back to sleep and even longer to get to deep sleep, and if I wake up too many times, I will not be able to achieve deep sleep.

Software engineering is a craft, and what you are crafting happens in your head. No amount of architecture drawings will be able to lift that cognitive load. The code Joe is writing is first built in his head, and as the fingers dance over the keyboard, he remembers all the variables, classes, and types in play. He mentally tells himself to remember to update some other library, but not now, as this will break the flow. He is like a circus juggler with both flaming torches and chainsaws. Therefore, you should be very careful not to pull Joe out of the zone. Not with meetings, not even with a "hi Joe – tell me what you're working on," even if that is quite a nice thing to ask if you are his manager.

Sometimes, several engineers can be in the zone together. Sometimes in pairs (called pair programming) or the entire team (mob programming). It would be best if you didn't try to force them into any of these – this depends entirely on the problem to be solved and the team constellation.

When a team collaborates with another entity – a person, another group, or a department – it requires an investment: The cognitive load increases as we need to understand the other entity for a fruitful collaboration. Cognitive load is, however, finite. Sometimes, the price of cognitive load is not worth it.

Consider when you just want to consume a service and when you want to invest in true collaboration. As an extreme example: I do not want to collaborate with my Water Supplier. I want to consume their service and get water when I turn it on. I do not need to collaborate on the filters they use to clean the water. I trust them, and I consume a service. You might have teams in your organization today with whom you collaborate at the cost of cognitive load, where you could benefit from one being a service provider and the other a consumer of said service.

That's how it is in Joe's team. Some teams provide an API to a service or some data, and Joe's team is pleased when the API is well documented and discoverable in the API gateway. An API is an Application Programming Interface. It is a way to tell the world what kind of data and functionality you expose and how you should behave if you want to get a hold of said data and functionality. APIs are a method of working together without the cognitive load of collaborating. Joe smiles when he thinks of this particular way of working. He and his engineering colleagues know it makes sense, and they communicate through APIs because they want to, not because they are forced to do so. Joe remembers that the boss of one of the biggest tech companies in the world wrote an email to his entire engineering population stating that they should communicate through APIs or

For a software development team, collaboration is a specific thing. It is a deliberate action with a dedicated purpose limited in time and space.

they would be fired. Joe would have quit immediately upon receiving this. Not because it is a bad idea, but because leading through mandates is a turn-off for software engineers.

Joe takes off his headphones and walks to the water cooler. To solve the problem he is working on, he needs to get the retail price of an item sold in the webshop he is building, but that price data belongs to another team, so he needs to get a hold of that data somehow. Joe knows it makes little

sense to get a copy of the database because that will be out-
dated the minute it is updated. He also knows the standard
way to handle cross-team collaboration is through APIs. Joe
hangs around at the water cooler a bit until spotting Laura.
He knows she is on the team that works with the prices and
has a question about the API the team exposes. Laura enjoys
the water cooler chat, and later they continue the conversa-
tion in the asynchronous chat software. He's happy that the
company only has one collaboration platform – otherwise it
would be hard to find and ask for information. Joe expects
his company to have a professional developer portal where
he can find APIs, SDKs, and accompanying documentation. Ideally, everything should be available in the developer
portal. The entire developer experience (DX) is significant
to all software engineers. It should be treated as any other
product, with user research, outcome-based focus, prioritization, and frequent user feedback loops. If you do not treat
DX as a product in your company, and throw resources after
it, chances are there are a lot of unhappy Joe's out there.

Joe grabs a piece of cake and his coffee and returns to the
computer to write more code. Much like when you are hi-
king in the wild, it is not the clock that determines when
it's time to stop for the day. Instead, it is the circumstances.
Is this a nice place to camp? Can I put up my tent here, and
is there a source for water and firewood? The same thing
happens to a software engineer. An excellent place to take
a break is if the "juggling" is over. All the items up in the
air have been put into the code, and the feature is ready to
be tested and committed.

Joe commits his code, and even though every unit test is green, he fires up his dashboard and looks at the various metrics. Does his code cause an increase in CPU or memory usage? What about network traffic? Everything looks fine, and Joe decides to hang out for a bit, reading his favorite websites and hoping to discuss a bit more with his colleagues at the fussball table. Joe meets his boss on his way to the car and is happy that the boss never makes any remarks (even jokingly) about when Joe decides to leave for the day.

Something about metrics

Joe is fond of metrics. An inner pleasure arises in seeing a number or a curve change based on your code. It adds an element of gamification to his job, and it motivates him. But measurement can be abused, and just as they motivate a software engineer, used badly, measures can demotivate. Unfortunately, this happens a lot, and Joe hopes that someday, someone will write a manual on how to keep software engineers motivated.

According to Joe, one of the misleading and demotivating factors is when someone mistakenly considers a measure for targets. Joe remembers his old teacher at the university telling a story, which he still thinks explains the problem very well. As far as he remembers, the story went something like this:

"In Spain, this small village made its primary income from tourism. They were known for being a place where old pottery of pristine quality was excavated, and this attracted a lot of tourists. Unfortunately, all the digging also attracted rats, so the city had two problems: they needed more pottery to attract tourists and fewer rats not to scare tourists away. The mayor of the town immediately thought about incentives. He was of the old school, not knowing the difference between intrinsic and extrinsic motivation. So, he launched two programs. The first program was to collect pieces of pottery – he awarded one coin to each part of pottery. He also awarded one coin for every rat killed.

The mayor was happy. He soon had a room filled with shards of pottery and a large container filled with dead rats.

Of course, what happened was that when the citizens found a pristine, undamaged piece of pottery, they broke it into pieces to get more coins.

And to maximize their coins, they started breeding rats."

The mayor didn't know that when a metric becomes a target, it ceases to be a good metric. This is known as Goodhart's Law, named after a British economist in the 1970s. Other names are Perverse Incentives or The Cobra Effect[5], named after an incident in India during British rule. The British government had serious apprehensions about the venomous cobras, so they offered a bounty for every dead cobra. This resulted in an increase in breeding cobras, leading to the bounty program's closure. The breeders set the cobras free, as they were now worthless, resulting in a massive increase in cobras in the wild.

Joe has seen way too often that unhealthy behavior arises when teams are suddenly incentivized by moving a specific measurement. Not only that – the metrics cease to be good metrics. He remembers one manager who incentivized teams with high velocity, which meant no team would spend time helping others, and the overall velocity went down as a result.

The second thing that demotivates Joe is when someone picks up the measurements and starts comparing teams – "team A is obviously better than team B – just look at the measurements." Creating software is an art just as much as it is a craft. Imagine if Van Gogh was called a better painter than Rembrandt because he used less paint or had more paint strokes per minute.

Joe's team loves LEGO bricks. Who doesn't? Based on LEGO bricks, his team has some very cool visualizations of their metrics. Here is a breakdown of the things they measure to become better.

Time to onboard a new colleague. Each brick is one week. Joe's team is growing, and they hire a lot of skilled colleagues. The new colleague needs a new computer with admin rights and the right software installed. She needs access to all the right services and to know where to find documentation, source code, tools, etc. They measure it from when

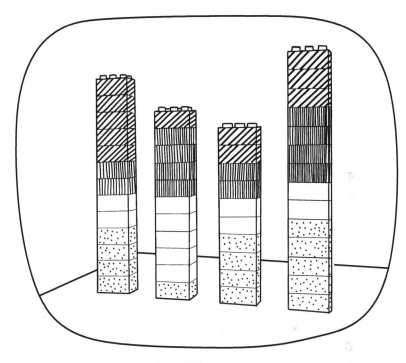

Four different teams

the colleague has the first working day to when the first piece of code is deployed to production.

Time from idea to a new service is live, in production. Each brick is one day. The team remembers the old days of stage-gate models and governance boards where it could take weeks or months to get a new service live. Now, all kind of governance is automated, and it makes sense to measure days, not months. This measurement is excellent because it will also show if there is inertia or bottlenecks in the system and the value stream from idea to production.

Check if my code builds and works. Each brick is a second.
This is hard to portray to non-engineers. But sometimes,
you make many small changes and want to compile, build,
and run quickly, just to check the behavior. Each engineer
does this every day, and it makes a massive difference if
it takes 10 seconds versus 10 minutes. To Joe, this would
probably be the most crucial metric that everyone should
care about.

**Does this change break governing constraints? Each brick
is one day.** In Joe's company, they take security and privacy
seriously, and there are a lot of nonfunctional requirements
(NFR). Not just security, but other forms as well. Valida-
ting if a change conforms to the large number of NFRs takes time, and Joe's team strives to make that time as short
as possible.

Time to validate a hypothesis; each brick is one week. Joe's
team welcomes any change from anyone, but they always
ask: "How will you know this is successful?" The answer
is usually some metric that will move. The team measures
the time it takes to validate if the change was beneficial or
not. Measuring the length of a feedback loop is a good idea
if you want to have as many meaningful feedback loops as
possible.

Joe's team does not mind showcasing the metrics together
with the other teams because there is no one trying to compare them and claiming one team is better than the other.
The team working closer to the customer has more NFRs

and a more complicated build mechanism because they build on multiple platforms, so of course, they have more bricks than the internal teams. But the teams only use these metrics to improve within the groups. They share the learning and the initiatives they have put in place to improve. They are happy if other teams can learn from them and happily learn from other teams.

The teams also measure the DevOps metrics (DORA – short for the DevOps Research and Assessment Team), which are four standardized metrics: How often does the team deploy to production (Deployment Frequency), the time it takes from code commit to deploy (Lead time for Change), the time it takes to fix it when something is broken (Mean time to Recovery) and the number of bad deployments (Change Failure Rate). These are great metrics because, after the success of the book Accelerate[6], many teams measure these specifically and are all familiar with them. They are trailing indicators – sometimes also called lagging indicators - because they can only be known after the event has happened.

It can sometimes be challenging to understand the difference between leading and lagging indicators, so here is an example:

Measure: Customer Satisfaction.
Metric: The yearly Customer Satisfaction survey.

This is a trailing indicator. You can only know how satisfied the customers are after they have had that feeling and you have measured customer satisfaction

A leading indicator of Customer Satisfaction could be: *The number of calls to Customer Service*; receiving a minimum number of calls would probably mean satisfied customers. This is a leading indicator.

DORA metrics are still great, even if they are trailing indicators, so long as the team uses the important leading indicators that Joe's team has created and you don't compare teams. Deploying a mobile app *will* take longer than deploying a web solution. You must comply with the app store in question depending on your target OS. For example, Apple does not allow native code updates on the fly (at the time of writing). To fix your code, you must submit a new build and go through the formal procedure. This is a security and quality decision from Apple, which you may agree with or not, but the fact of the matter is that it can take days for the teams' code to get to production, and you cannot reasonably compare an App team with a Web team or similar.

Like team metrics, Joe also enjoys it when the product he is working on has metrics. It feels good to launch some code that moves a metric. Product metrics are also challenging to define; even well-defined healthy metrics can lose value. For example, back in the day, web teams measured page views, average time spent on site, session length, etc. These metrics used to be great when web browsing was done in a single web browser on a computer. Today, most web browsing is done in tabs, across several devices, expecting single-page apps dynamically loading with some nice react.js code. This effectively nullifies many old "workhorse" metrics because a page might be dormant in a tab while the user does something else. There are still some suitable measures left, though. Like the evergreen DAU/MAU (Daily Active Unique-Users, Monthly Active Unique-Users). However, they cannot be used without context. A well-funded marketing campaign can boost the DAU. If the team is unaware of what marketing activities are taking place for their digital real estate, they can't know if the growth is genuinely organic.

The team must understand why a specific metric makes sense. If the team works on an e-commerce site, monthly sales growth should be an excellent metric for them, right? After all, if the team can make a better search functionality or a smoother check-out flow, sales should go up. While that is true, other things impact sales as well. The prices might be adjusted down, causing an increase in the number of items sold. The prices might be increased, causing a decrease in the number of items sold. The product might be featured in a popular TV series, causing a massive spike in interest. The point here is that such a metric is only valid if all related metrics are presented alongside it, showing the necessary context.

Product metrics should be so attractive that they are scrutinized weekly. They are presented on product review days and are immediately recognizable; it is evident what a change up or down indicates. They are comparative over time – for

instance, "X has improved 6% compared to the same pe-
riod last year". Finally, metrics are not goals. They are not
something you simply must achieve. A good product metric
represents a hypothesis that the team wants to validate. It
is just as valuable to learn that something is not working
as it is to understand that something is working. Product
metrics are not just beneficial for the product teams and
the company. They are also valuable for the team working
on creating or improving the product.

Business apophenia – how to make sense of it all

Vision – the ability to see – is a wonderful sense to have. As we look at something, light enters the eye through a lens, focusing the light on the retina. From here, the optic nerve begins sending signals back through the brain. Like all other senses, they need to pass the thalamus, which relays the signals to the visual cortex, located in the back of the brain. The actual process is a bit more complicated than this – we have a visual cortex and a primary visual cortex, the optic chiasm, and other parts, but let's stay with the simple model for this analogy. Signals enter the eyes and are sent through "pipes" to the visual cortex. Think of the pipes as bandwidth. The more pipes, the more information can be sent to the visual cortex. The fun thing is that the number of pipes *from* the visual cortex is a factor ten of the pipes going *in*. We are not just reacting to things we see but also to something we predict. And in fact, we are responding to a factor ten on our ability to predict what we actually see.

If we had to react and sense everything, our brain couldn't do anything else. Walking down a road, we don't need to spend energy watching every step. We can predict how it will go and be walking, thinking about something else. That is until we reach the woods where the ice hasn't been removed. It's an icy path with roots and other slippery obstacles on it. We need to sense every step, and suddenly, we need to use the total inward capacity. Then, back on the paved road, we can skip the sensory input and base our movement on prediction. Our brain loves to do that. The more it can rely on forecasts, the more it can use capacity on something else.

Our brain is often seen as a pattern-matching machine. It loves to see and predict patterns everywhere. We have all heard about people seeing the image of Jesus in a piece of

toast. We can see faces and figures in clouds. In the image below, we can clearly see a triangle, even though it is just three rotations of Pac man.

This is called apophenia, and while the phenomenon has been known to humankind for the past 50,000 years, it wasn't until 1958 that a term was coined. The German psychiatrist Klaus Conrad defined apophenia as "unmotivated seeing of connections accompanied by a specific feeling of meaningfulness[7]." Apophenia is not limited to images or sound; it is also used to describe behavioral patterns such as *the Gambler's fallacy,* where we are inclined to think that if we toss a coin and it lands five times in a row with heads up, surely there is a higher probability of it being tail side up at the next toss.

Apophenia in business is the common denominator for the various antipatterns that have come to exist due to a wrong interpolation of data points. These antipatterns arise for various reasons – maybe the data was correct, but the interpolation was terrible. Or the data was incorrect, but the interpolation was accurate. As with other examples of apophenia, the phenomenon's strength increases with the frequency of experience. It can be hard to argue against a belief that roots in apophenia. In 2004 a woman got a grilled cheese that she thought looked like the Virgin Mary. While most people would say this is just our pattern-matching brain playing tricks with us, she firmly believed in it. And so did many others, as the grilled piece of cheese was sold for a premium price at an online auction.

Similarly, we encounter business apophenia in many places, which can be just as hard to counter. Creating and measuring output has been the cornerstone of project management for years and is still taught in courses today. This means we have managers trained in this behavior employing people with a similar school of thought. In the same courtyard, we have the dichotomy of "thinkers" and "doers" from Scientific Management[8]. The idea is that we have intelligent people – the thinkers – designing and describing the work to be done by the not-so-smart doers. Because this way of working is effective in the simple and even in the complicated domain, it naturally flows into the complex domain.

The critical thing to understand here is that even if we understand all the principles outlined in this book, we will meet resistance and face business apophenia. Not due to malice or stupidity, but because the current behavior has been natural to these people. It has made sense. To understand this sense-making, we can use the process from "Sensemaking in Organizations," where Karl Weick describes it as a set of properties[9].

1. **Identity:** Who people think they are, shapes the way they act. Henceforth, if you think you are a "thinker" and identify yourself as such, then surely you would not empower a team to deliver an outcome; you will immediately establish a steering committee of thinkers to set a direction for the doers.

2. **Time of retrospection:** The point where people look back at the impacts of the learning. In "classic" projects, you do an After-Action Review and review the project after completion, while in Agile, you conduct a retrospective after each sprint.

3. **Enacting narratives:** As people speak and build narratives around themselves, they act by this narrative. This is a complexity-reducing factor because it makes communication more fluent if the discourse has been honed within the narrative. The Identity property further increases this. By talking to and identifying with, other people of a similar role, the narrative will be even more homogeneous.

4. **Sense-making is a social activity:** Stories are told and live in the social circles that create them. There is no audience to contradict or react to the stories told. Linking directly to the point above, the narratives are shared and retained by the people making them.

5. **Sense-making is an ongoing process:** While retrospectives might be discrete, sense-making constantly happens, constantly replenishing the beliefs.

6. **Extracting cues:** People extract cues from the context to help them decide if a piece of information is relevant or not. Combined with point four above, this means that there is a high probability of an echo chamber effect, simply because if a piece of information doesn't fit in a

narrative, it is discarded. Weick has a great example with a platypus. When scientists first found the remains of a platypus, they were stumped. It had a beak, an otter's body, a beaver's tail, and feet like a duck. They couldn't make sense of this, so they simply omitted some facts for this animal to fit into their picture of the world.

7. **Plausibility over accuracy:** We tend to favor what is plausible rather than correct. Especially when it comes to sensemaking, we are inclined to believe something as soon as we deem it plausible. This works hand in hand with the point about extracting cues. We simply gather information until it is sufficient to consider our belief credible.

In business, there is a belief that the company has a stable state. In biology, this is called homeostasis – a condition where the entire organism functions optimally. The temperature is just right. The blood glucose level is on point, and our fluid levels are balanced. Our body has systems that regulate this through hormones. The renin-angiotensin system regulates blood pressure and electrolyte balances through hormones. The pancreas regulates blood glucose levels through the hormone insulin. Homeostasis is predictive. If a person consumes carbohydrates, the blood glucose level rises, and in turn, the pancreas releases insulin, causing the glucose level to even out again. If you have a homeostatic belief as a company, you would be inclined to establish similar control functions controlling the system's regulators. The challenge begins when the system is disturbed by external factors, causing instability. In biology, *allostasis* is sometimes used to describe the process of achieving stability through physiological or behavioral change. Allostasis comes from the Greek "allo," which means "variable," representing "remaining stable by being variable." Of course, this is just an analogy – a business is not an organic system. However, some transformational learning is embedded in thinking about the company as a body to weed out the apophenia and status-quo thinking that might have emerged through the years.

With the globalization of businesses and workforces, the ability and agility to react to external influences are becoming more relevant. A century ago, your business competition was likely close to you. It might be a competing bakery or a blacksmith setting up shop in the nearby town. Now, competitors can emerge worldwide and come from various industries. The hotel owner is no longer worried about a new Hilton being built in the city – the competitor is an app called Airbnb that serves the same "job to be done" without carrying the weight of owning multiple properties. Smartphones, not other camera companies, are challenging the camera companies. We are entering a world where apophenia and homeostasis can severely impact the company's future.

One way to counter rigid group-thinking that has slowly grown in many organizations is introducing diversity into the workforce—diversity at all levels and in as many parameters as possible. As evident by looking at organizations today, diversity does not come free. It requires work because humans tend to group with people like themselves – what is known as homophily – expressed by the sentence "birds of a feather flock together." It is often seen that managers hire people that reflect their own beliefs and appearance, and when people make new acquaintances, the first thing they do is to look for similarities. People they both know, education they share, movies they've seen, etc. The problem with homophily is that it creates collective blindness.

If a team consists of similar team members, none of them will see what they are not seeing.

As with anything that is part of human nature, it requires an intervention to change, and homophily is a part of human nature.

The evidence of the power of diversity is substantial. It is fragmented across multiple scientific areas, but there's a relatively strong attraction toward psychology. For instance, the article "Culture and point of view"[10] provides an insight into the differences between the east and the west. It challenges the assumption that the fundamental processes of cognition and perception are universal and that inductive and deductive inference, attention, memory, categorization, and causal analysis are the same for everyone in every culture. The article then cites some quite exciting studies. Groups from different backgrounds are asked to memorize and classify pictures, showing how differing cultural backgrounds mean they pay attention to different parts of the pictures.

But the exciting result in the spirit of diversity is that when you group the different backgrounds, the ability to recall the pictures increases dramatically. None of the homogenous groups performed as well as the group of people with different backgrounds.

The same pattern is found by Scott Page[11], a professor at the University of Michigan. Pages' results are interesting because he initially set out to motivate his students by proving that the best and the brightest would perform the best. However, as his research progressed, he eventually proved that the more diverse team would outperform the more capable teams if the problem were complex enough. This means that if the problem is "simple," such as "solve this integral equation," a group of mathematicians would outperform the diverse group. The key learning here is that diversity is a differentiator when the problems are complex – or wicked.

Why aren't we actively doing more to create diverse teams in the presence of scientific evidence? One reason might be that a diverse team initially feels less confident in their ability to perform. In the article "Is the pain worth the gain," Phillips et al. l[12] dive into the impact of diversity. While they reach the same conclusions regarding the ability to increase performance, they bring a new aspect to the table. Namely, groups with out-group newcomers (i.e., diverse groups) reported less confidence in their performance. They perceived their interactions as less effective. Yet, they performed better than groups with in-group newcomers (i.e., homogeneous groups). Moreover, performance gains were not due to newcomers bringing new ideas to the group discussion. Instead, the results demonstrate that the mere presence of socially distinct newcomers and the social concerns their presence stimulates among existing members motivates behavior that can convert affective pains into cognitive gains.

We also see consulting companies entering the field. The signals showing that the diversity train is rolling are that the big consulting companies are picking it up and that the investment world is 'investing' in diversity. Both of these are happening. In the article "Ethnic diversity deflates price bubbles," Levine et al. dive into the aspect of price bubbles that arise when trades collectively err in pricing. They hypothesized that this is due to ethnic homogeneity and conducted an experiment showing that ethnically diverse groups are less likely to make the same pricing errors.

Cognitive diversity means a broader palette of problem-solving skills when attacking a problem. Just as a neural network requires many different nodes with different weights, a team of humans needs different perspectives, drawing on various data sources and experiences.

The point to remember here is that 'diversity' is a complex term. Try not to get lured into the trap of making it mean something specific just because it is easy to measure. Try not to measure diversity by numbers or ratios, and do not discriminate. Do not fall into the trap of requiring your staff to speak or act in a certain way[13]. Be an open and inclusive workplace through your actions and procedures. Recognize that diversity in and of itself is not a goal. Some teams need to be more homogeneous than others. It all depends on what they do and who they are. If you are an inclusive workplace, diversity will follow. Your first step toward diversity therefore begins with inclusivity.

Working on wicked problems

A problem is wicked if there is no single solution to the problem. It can be better, or it can be worse, but it can't be solved.

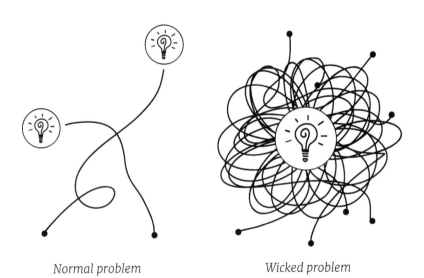

Normal problem   Wicked problem

Being diagnosed with diabetes is wicked because there is no cure, but there are various ways of making your life better – or worse. However, once science proves that a cure can be found, the problem is no longer wicked. A less draconian example is a social media app. It is impossible to say, "build me a social network app and let me know when it's done." It's never done, but initiatives and new features make the product better or worse. People don't use social media because of its features. They use them because it enables them to connect socially. New privacy laws are constantly seeing the light of day, and new competing social networks arise almost daily. It is impossible to make a list of features and say that the app is done once the engineers have built these features. The engineers must continuously build things, measure the effects, cultivate learning, rinse, and repeat. The product managers must be exact in describing the desired outcomes and leave the outputs to the teams.

A product is what the team delivers. A product can be something physical (like a phone), it can be software (like Microsoft Word), or it can be a service (like teaching or nursing).

In classic scrum, there is a role defined called a product owner. This role is defined in the scrum guide as:

- Clearly expressing Product Backlog items.
- Ordering the items in the Product Backlog to best achieve goals and missions.

- Optimizing the value of the work the Development Team performs.
- Ensuring that the Product Backlog is visible, transparent, and clear to all.

In many organizations, this role is the person leading the product. However, reading the definition, it is clear that this role is "just" the person doing the prioritization and sequencing of the list of things to be done - in scrum, called a 'backlog.' This led to the emergence of a new role called a product manager. In his excellent book Inspired, Marty Cagan defines the product manager in great detail[14]. He coins the product manager as the mini-CEO of the product - an exceptional talent with the potential to lead the entire company. The product manager (PM) needs to ensure business viability and user value, which in turn means that the PM should have deep knowledge of the industry and the consumers/customers of the product. The product manager works with the entire product lifecycle from product discovery to delivery to optimization, constantly cycling through these phases in short feedback loops. It is the PM's accountability to handle risks of all kinds: Can we afford the solution? Does the solution we're looking into work for our partners? Is it consistent with our brand? Can we even sell it, and are our channels equipped to do so? Can we do it legally? What about ethics? And do we have the know-how and capabilities to do it?

There are many other definitions of product managers out there. While they are all great suggestions, there is a problem with defining the product manager/product owner, which is the discourse and presuppositions in using the word "product." Let's explore:

Imagine a small country consisting of two islands. Over the years, the island's population has skewed, and there are more people on one island than the other. The obvious solution would be to redistribute the density by allowing people to travel between the islands.

We can define an outcome: 'An inhabitant can cross the water with dry feet.' Now, the product delivering on this outcome might be a boat. But it might also be a bridge. Two different outputs require vastly different skill sets to build, operate and maintain.

Most product owner role descriptions are about that specific output, but what happens when the boat has reached maximum capacity and it would make more sense to build a bridge?

Who takes the lead and states that we need new capabilities? We need to learn engineering and bridge-building skills. Is this only the role of a leader, or is this something anyone can do?

The role that the organization needs is someone "leading the problem." While the product owner is part of the team, this role has to live outside the team. The reason is that it will not be the same team delivering the bridge as it is delivering the boat. The self-preservation mechanism inherent in all teams will force them to keep optimizing the boat, making it faster, bigger and better when the correct solution is to build a bridge.

The question is who takes a holistic view of the situation and makes the tough decisions. It is not a product owner. Nor is it a project manager or a program manager. It's someone who cares deeply about the outcome - in the example case - crossing a river with dry feet. Someone that is sufficiently detached from the various solutions to remain unbiased. Even separated from the outcome, revisiting that regularly. The ones having the problem are the customers or, in this example, the islands' inhabitants. There is not one person who owns the problem but rather *a customer* or *a market*. Both are very fluffy entities. The idea here is to apply sense-making and sense what product or service the market needs. Or even sense what/who the market is. It's not just about product discovery. It's about customer discovery. Find a market. Figure out their problem. Solve said problem. Phrased as a science experiment, it is about creating a hypothesis that can prove or disprove some observation through a series of experiments. This must happen in short feedback loops as the market, problems, and solutions constantly fluctuate.

The learning here is that the product is an artifact of solving the problem. Moving people from one island to the other is the problem. One product that solves this is a boat. Another product that solves this is a bridge. Global warming may cause the water to evaporate, and a boat is no longer sustainable. Maybe a shortage of a critical component in boat motors means we all need to take the bridge for a while. The crucial point is that we do not know what the future will bring. We need to probe, sense, and respond.

We observe many companies organizing in product teams and structuring their portfolio around these products. While this works in a stable environment with non-wicked problems, it is not optimal in a complex world with emerging problems and changing conditions. Digital products must be considered artifacts of a wicked problem, and there are alternatives to product teams. Instead, think of teams as stable, long-lived capability teams, and instead of moving people to products, let problems flow to teams. Like metal shards aligning to a magnet, these teams can align to a workstream or a platform. There are plenty of details on this way of organizing, very well described in the book Team Topologies[15].

Motivating through outcomes

Consider the following leadership aspiration. Your job as a leader is to:

"Ensure employee's long-term motivation for them to deliver value continuously."

We want a healthy system, and the health of a system consisting of knowledge workers can be measured by their motivation. The case for choosing motivation as a metric consists of several sub-parts. Motivated employees stay longer; it is expensive to hire and train a new employee in most organizations. Motivated employees produce better work, especially if they are knowledge workers like software engineers. "Motivate" stems from *motus*, which means to move, and a motivated person is someone who is moved to do something. The dichotomy of motivation is distilled, black and white. You are either motivated to do something that brings you pleasure, or you are motivated to do something that

moves you away from pain. Whipping captured enemies to row a boat is a motivator. Management by fear is a motivator. The fear of losing your job is a powerful motivator and an easy lever to pull. However, there is another dichotomy of motivation. Intrinsic and extrinsic types of motivation or internal and external motivation. These two interoperate with each other, and it suffices to say that your internal motivation decreases if the external motivator is negative. There is a nice touch on intrinsic vs. extrinsic motivation in an article by Ryan & Deci[16], where they conclude that contextual social conditions that support one's feelings of competence, autonomy, and relatedness are the basis for one maintaining intrinsic motivation and becoming more self-determined with respect to extrinsic motivation. The facilitation of conditions that satisfy these three basic human needs —to support the innate needs to feel connected, effective, and authentic as one is exposed to new ideas and exercises new skills.

Motivation is like energy. You can't see it, but you can see the effects of it. If you move a magnet over a tabletop with iron filings, you will see the shards move and arrange themselves. While you cannot see the magnetic field, you can see what happens if it's there. It is also evident that nothing happens if you wave a banana over the shards instead of a magnet.

Similarly, if you wave a magnet over popcorn, nothing happens either. We can make some exciting observations if we accept this as an analogy for motivation. While we cannot see motivation, just as we can't see energy, we can directly see the result of the presence of energy or motivation. In classic physics, energy is divided into potential energy and kinetic energy. Potential energy is "internal" in the sense that a rock can have energy if it is lifted in the air. Once dropped, it will release this energy into movement, heat, or both. Kinetic energy is "external" because if a rock moves at a certain speed, we can directly calculate the energy as a function of the mass and the rock's velocity. You cannot see energy, but you can see the consequences of energy, and you can use energy, just like motivation.

Motivation is like energy. You can't see it, but you can see the effects of it.

Long-term motivation means that it's not enough to just be nice. Buying the employees ice cream and sending them home might cater for the short term, but chances are they would be replaced by someone more capable in the long run. This means the 'long term' links directly to 'continuously deliver value.'

If we, for a moment, accept that 'value' means whatever we think it means, what do we mean by "continuously?" The word means "without interruption, not stopping." If our system needs to 'not stop' delivering value, learning and continuous improvement must be built into the system. With methods that are no longer contemporary, value delivery will halt or decrease. If we are not learning, our methods will become obsolete or deprecated at some point. Therefore, learning and value delivery are directly linked.

If you do not include learning in whatever value metric you create, your teams will eventually stall.

"If you do what you've always done, you will get the results you've always gotten." That inscription is seen on plaques and motivational posters everywhere as a friendly push to break old habits. The problem is that it is not a true statement. "The Red Queen" effect tells us that if we do what we have always done, we will get fewer results than we've always gotten. The Red Queen effect is named after a section in "Through the Looking Glass," – the sequel to "Alice in Wonderland." Alice asks the Queen why she is always running so fast, and the Queen says: "Look at my surroundings – they are all moving as fast as we are now. To get ahead, we must run even faster than our surroundings". If we do not learn and increase our mental capacity as an organization, we will fall victim to the Red Queen effect.

Let us return to 'value.' What do we mean when we talk about value? In short, it is all about the *outcome*, not the *output*. At first, the two terms might seem interchangeable, but there is a massive difference in this context. Consider the following examples:

OUTPUT	OUTCOME
A successful abdominal surgery	The patient no longer has pain from an infected appendix
Implementation of the new Buy Master 2000 e-commerce system	Online sales have increased by 14%
A complete re-organization of the entire division.	Productivity and motivation are up.
Implementation of a new cashier system	Waiting times decreased by 50%

Table 1: Difference between output and outcome

The output on the left might very well have produced the outcome on the right, which is why we, for many years, have trained project managers in tracking output – simply because output and outcome often are closely related. If we become obsessed with delivering value, we need to become obsessed with delivering an outcome. This means we ask the team to deliver the desired outcome, not the output. Sometimes, the team will achieve the outcome by other means than first assumed. Imagine the delight if they achieve the outcome by working less, not more. Maybe the patient in the first example did not need to have their appendix removed. Perhaps the IT system was not responsible for the

e-commerce sales in example two. Maybe the reorganiza-
tion in example three was not necessary.

Software engineers love to deliver excellent outcomes, and
they love to learn new things. They might be *satisfied* by
money, job perks, and bonuses, but those are all extrinsic,
and satisfaction differs from motivation.

To keep your engineers motivated, make sure they work on
something that makes sense. Like the old analogy – "I'm
not laying bricks, I'm building a cathedral." Make sure they
work in a learning organization and can continuously hone
their craft. And make sure they work in an empowered,
self-organizing team without too much bureaucracy.

This is often easier said than done, so here are a few concrete examples.

Avoid top-down architecture decisions. Try to avoid a dedicated software architect role. Software architecture is not
a title; it's something you do as part of software engineering. Just as there probably should not be a scrum master
title – it's something you do as part of working with the
scrum framework. Two things will happen if you have software architects at any level telling the teams what the right
architecture is. The obvious demotivating factor of taking
away a natural piece of software engineering from a team is
one thing. The other thing is that it will limit organizational
learning or even install what is known as "learned helplessness." If someone is always telling you the right thing to

do, what is the incentive for you to learn the right thing? It's so much easier to sit back and follow orders.

Try to make strategic decisions that influence architecture instead. Good architecture is about all the non-trivial technical choices that we make. Leadership can help move some of the decisions if they make the digital strategy clear. Good architecture will follow. Top-down architecture decisions will install learned helplessness or demotivate the teams even if they are the right decision, and much worse if they are the wrong decisions.

Work is work

Work is work. Digital teams are often organized into product teams, with a product owner/product manager prioritizing the backlog. The backlog is the list of user stories the team should work on. This has proven to be a great way of working, but there is an antipattern that needs some extra focus. Ideally and conceptually, work flows to the team through the backlog. The backlog is prioritized, so the teams work on what brings the most value, and it is easy to visualize if a team is working on more than one story. The problem arises when work flows into the team through channels other than the backlog. The enterprise architecture team might require all teams to switch to a new container platform. It might be the security team requiring all teams to implement a new control to deal with new legislation. Even finance and HR bring work to teams – maybe not software development, but they might ask them to report on hours spent, cloud usage cost, or the number of externals employed on the team. Anything a team must spend time on is considered work. This, of course, also includes meetings. Doing big transformational projects can severely impede a team and can heavily impact motivation. The product manager expects the team to work on problems or opportunities that will directly affect the end user. Still, the team might be forced to upgrade some systems or switch to a new type of virtual machine as part of a transformation. The pattern to replace this antipattern with is a strategic prioritization process. A digital team will inevitably be required to work on things not originating with the product manager, but a well-functioning team still needs priorities. Any work packages must be compared to the value that user stories on the backlog create and must be prioritized equally. Eventually, all work needs to end up in one backlog; otherwise, the team will lose focus and flow, but non-functional requirements (NFR) do not magically appear or get prioritized appropriately.

Technical debt is not like any other debt

As I read through the pages of the book I've written so far, I realized that some parts of it could have been written better. Some chapters should have been merged into one. Other chapters are of lower quality and should probably have been completely rewritten or even omitted. Other chapters have a strong point buried deep within the paragraphs, and the point will likely be missed.

I could fix all that by rewriting the whole or parts of this book. This is a 'debt' that I owe, but I could not have known what the debt was if I hadn't been writing the text in the first place.

As a matter of fact, the above paragraphs were written after two rewrites of the book. But I still have 'technical debt' – a term coined by one of the creators of the agile manifesto – Ward Cunningham. Writing a book can take forever

– something can constantly be improved. The same thing happens with software.

The term "technical debt" could probably benefit from being reframed into something more precise. We usually know 'debt' from the financial world. I owe you X. That's my debt. If I repay you X, then I no longer have a debt. In software, I might owe you 2*X after I repay you, so it works nothing like financial debt.

What's the value of rewriting this chapter on technical debt? Will I sell more books? It's hard to quantify and thus hard to prioritize. This unclear definition can make it hard to prioritize the effort it takes to work on technical debt.

With software, it can help to avoid bundling technical debt into pieces of work and instead work on a practice of continuous refactoring – something the team constantly works on. Sometimes, it will feel like delicately trimming small parts of a fragile bonsai tree; other times, it will feel like running a bulldozer through a landfill.

The value created by refactoring/reducing technical debt can be measured in various ways. One is through "fitness functions17." A fitness function measures how close a design is to achieving its primary function. Let's say you are working on a search engine. Ideally, most queries should respond fast with clear results. The "fast" past can be measured, so you could have a fitness function saying: "Time to get the result of a query should be less than 5 milliseconds".

The fitness function will be green if most queries are below that threshold. Refactoring your codebase could mean that more fitness functions will be green. Of course, not all software can have a fitness function, and other measures will also be used. The important thing is that the team must define them and own them.

Sometimes, it can make sense to centralize functionality, and sometimes it makes sense to duplicate functionality. As the saying goes – "it depends." If you are creating something user-facing – like a login functionality or profile page – it makes sense to only have one internal product that does this. Anything else might confuse the end user. Other functionalities, predominantly internal, can be duplicated if it enables flow. Centralizing a product will create a single point of failure, many dependencies, and, last but not least, a lot of coordination. All the users of this product will now have to coordinate with this single product and get their needed functionality prioritized and implemented. The thing to be aware of is whether the cost of delay and the cost of synchronization is higher than the cost of duplicating the product. If that is the case, and if the product is not handling enterprise-wide data objects, then duplication of effort could result in increased flow due to reduced dependencies. Don't fall into the trap of mandating that software should only be built once. It might initially make sense from a financial perspective, but in the long run, it can be more expensive and limit flow.

That doesn't mean you shouldn't make your products

available for the entire company to use through an API, but it shouldn't be done without strategic intent. The idea of distributed systems is not new. Notably, we saw the rise of the CORBA back in 1991. CORBA was the "Common Object Request Broker Architecture." An attempt to enable clients and servers to talk to each other in a neutral language, allowing each to be written in whatever language they wanted. This was a massive step toward distributed systems, and soon after SOAP was born. SOAP is the "Simple Object Access Protocol," which introduced a standard way of communicating between services (XML), and the talk of Service Oriented Architecture began. With the rise of the .com wave in 2000, REST APIs were born, fixing some of the weaknesses of SOAP. At first look, REST APIs were a huge deal. You would not only know how to call the API, but it would also tell you how to use the response. With this, organizations started to talk about 'breaking up the monolith,' splitting their extensive monolithic systems into microservices.

Basically, a REST interface is a phone number. You call the number, ask for the "recipe for cinnamon buns," and a well-formed response will be returned to you. Soon, your entire system will be a spider's web of services - and herein lies a problem. First of all, what happens if someone isn't picking up the phone? The recipe server is down. Or even worse, the server returning the price for the asset you are trying to sell on your e-commerce website is not responding. No one would be able to purchase anything, and if that is your entire business, you have a serious problem. Some smart people have thought about this and introduced asynchronous APIs. This means that the data will flow to a 'middleman,' enabling you to get the data even if no one is picking up the phone. Once the server is up again, it can update the message bus holding the data, which everyone who wants to use it can subscribe to. Of course, services can still go down or produce the wrong result, which is why critical digital products have engineers on call. That means you can call them to fix a problem, even on the weekends. Having synchronous REST APIs will mean almost everyone would be on call, even the teams not necessarily owning a critical "must be up" product, because the "must be available" product uses functionality that this team exposes. Asynchronous APIs solve some of this, but it is still a considerable cost and a risk that could be mitigated by duplicating services to minimize dependencies. Asynchronous APIs have the property that they are "eventually consistent" as opposed to "always consistent." This is also something to consider.

The preferred way to think is with a value aspect. Some call this API Economy. This essentially means that a team is aware of the positive economic effect this API has on the organization's profitability. This profitability is not just top line. It could also be cost avoidance – "if I build this API, then I know at least X teams will benefit from consuming it because they would not have to create the functionality themselves." The more teams that can benefit from consuming an API instead of coding functionality themselves, the more time can be spent on developing features and benefits for the customers.

APIs that handle and transfer rich data or a considerable amount of data are usually in high demand. Primarily because of the data aspect – rich data should never be duplicated – even if it reduces flow because data inconsistency will eventually decrease flow down the road. Some data also requires a lot of governance and security scrutiny, which other teams would love not to spend their time on. Especially if the API is externally exposed and contains personal, financial, or other sensitive data, the number of security controls required should never be duplicated but handled centrally.

A well-balanced API economy with a continuously refactored codebase and a focus on flow will help reduce technical debt organically.

Time not spent on removing technical debt can be used for innovation, if you have already defined what innovation means for your business. In the next chapter, you will meet a word you have seen before, but in a context you probably haven't considered.

13

Emergency – the innovation muscle that requires attention

The majority of our leadership body of knowledge stems from the experiences we have accumulated in a world that was primarily complicated. With the increase in complexity, it is only natural to question whether our leadership models have evolved sufficiently and adequately.

In a complicated world, the unknowns are known. You know what it is you don't know or don't have, and it is possible to create a plan to gain the knowledge or produce the product. In the complicated world, we can optimize and plan and improve, and Fredrick Taylor had a point and a place with his 1911 book Principles of Scientific Management.

Around the same time, another scientist was working with something completely different. In a small laboratory in the city of Wuerzburg, Professor Wilhelm Röntgen discovered something unusual. Crystals on his desk near his current experiment suddenly started to glow. Röntgen was working with a cathode ray tube, and while the fluorescence was not what he was working towards, he became curious about what was emerging in front of him. He tried to cover his tube with some heavy black paper, yet the rays seemed to be still able to pass through. Röntgen got a wild idea and tested it to see if it could pass through human flesh (being a man of his time, he did not use his own hand – instead, he experimented on his wife's hand, of course). And with that, one of the most significant discoveries in medical science was made. Not because anyone was looking for it, but because it had emerged out of a sense of curiosity. It had emerged because Röntgen allowed himself to look at a pattern he did not expect instead of immediately discarding it.

Some years later, Scottish physician Alexander Flemming returned from a holiday to discover mold on a discarded petri dish that was preventing the expected bacteria around it from growing. Not knowing what this was or why it had happened, Flemming followed his curiosity and started to explore the mold with his students. Thus, another invention saw the light of day as penicillin and took its rightful place in our medical toolbox.

Wilson Greatbatch put the wrong resistors into an oscillator, and the pacemaker emerged. Constantin Fahlberg accidentally got some coal tar residue in his mouth and noticed it tasted sweet and, in turn, invented the artificial sweetener saccharin.

The list goes on.

If it weren't for emergence, we would not have potato chips, coca cola, microwaves, and chocolate chip cookies.

However, emergency as a word and concept is nowhere to be found in modern leadership.

When we see the word emergency, we tend to think of a medical emergency, i.e., an accident has happened. And the terms "accidental" and "emergency" are quite firmly linked in our brains.

Nothing is preventing us from de-linking them and allowing for emergency to be used in a positive sense. Instead, training organizations to be observant of weak patterns emerging from the complexity of our everyday world.

How might leadership help cultivate emergency in organizations? Or maybe the question should be phrased otherwise: What kind of leadership behavior prevents emergency, and are there behaviors that support emergency?

In the complicated world where the unknowns are known, clarity is a good thing. A leader who knows how to optimize a process and lead the work to perfection within time, scope, and budget is good—a leader who invades the production space and spots imperfections and process improvement possibilities with laser eyes. The space invader removes waste by eliminating anything that doesn't immediately show value. The space invader brings a great toolbox of best practices and is fluent in lean, six sigma, and balanced scorecards. And to make it abundantly clear – there is nothing wrong with this. The world needs space invaders, and this kind of leadership has saved many a factory. However, many an opportunity has been killed by the space invader, and another type of leadership is coming.

There is a need for individuals to be curious about emergency. In the complex world, where the unknowns are unknown, forcing clarity will inevitably hinder innovation. That is why Flemming picked up the proverbial discarded petri dish. That is why Percy Spencer was interested in why his chocolate bar was melting when working with certain kinds of microwaves.

Creating the space nurturing the curiosity to follow emergencies is called Agency. While the word is used in many

Forcing clarity will inevitably hinder innovation

different arenas, we use it here in the sociological terminology, where agency defines individuals' capacity and capability to act independently.

Agency is also used in psychology but in a slightly different context. In psychology, agents are usually attributed to intent. While the behavior is the same – that agency is the capability and capacity of autonomy, the context of intent and goal direction is different.

The "agency" we will describe here is not necessarily attributed to a specific goal, but more the autonomy to detect weak patterns and go with the emergent discovery, even if this does not necessarily bring the agent closer to a pre-defined goal or success criteria.

The space evader is a leader that evades the white space between tasks, operations, and relations. The leader creates the optimal space for agency to thrive and emergent innovation to live.

Leadership and power – name it to tame it

In 1956, Dwight D. Eisenhower said: "*Farming is easy when your plow is a pencil, and you're 1000 miles away from the field*". This could be read as follows: "Bring decision-making power to the people who understand the problem instead of bringing a problem to the people with decision-making power."

A lot of organizations are growing these days. It may be in size or complexity, or it could grow in product offerings or portfolio range. Whatever parameters are in play, the leadership role will change because the underlying "system" is changing to cope with the growth. The change might be organic and uncontrolled, or it might be deliberate. Chances are, it is both because the system will most likely react to the circumstances it finds itself in, whether these are caused deliberately by management or outside events.

The system will need to be more closely defined to explore this further. Humberto Maturana uses the term autopoiesis from Greek αὐτο- (auto-), meaning "self," and ποίησις (poiesis), meaning "creation, production," which states that any system is self-creating and has an inherent ability to create and re-invent itself. While the term originated in biology, it has found its way into organizations, primarily credited to Niklas Luhman. One of Luhman's statements was that although the system can use and rely on resources outside the system, those resources are not part of the system. In this context, the system is your organization, interacting with other systems and being influenced by other systems. The leader is part of the autopoiesis constantly taking place.

In this context, leadership is defined as "what capabilities the system requires to function." In that sense, even calling it leadership might be stretching it too much because there might not be any systemic needs for "a leader," nor do we know if leadership as we know it is required for the system to function optimally. However, in this context, it is a basic assumption that a leader will need to perform some role, and what remains is a curiosity about what that role might be.

The system that the leader role will live in is an autopoietic system. It is constructed by everybody – the team members, the products, the leaders, and everything in it.

This means, in turn, that the entire system shapes the leader's role. The idea of having an organic view of the system is not new. As already mentioned, Luhman introduced it more than 30 years ago. However, the explanation for why we ended up here is relatively novel. In his book "Reinventing Organizations[18]," Frederic Laloux looks back through humankind and maps human consciousness with how we organize. He uses the light spectrum to give these organizations names, starting with "organization zero," labeled 'red.' A red organization is a constant exercise of power by a strong alpha to keep the pack in line. The organization complies out of fear of repercussion from the alpha. Such an organization is highly reactive with a short-term focus and thrives in chaotic environments.

The leader role is shaped by the entire system.

The next level is 'amber' with highly formal roles within a hierarchical structure. Here we find the top-down command and control culture on "the what" and "the how," with rigorous processes and governance. Evolving from that comes 'orange' with the simple goal of achieving profit and growth. Innovation is the key to staying ahead. We then find the 'green' organization. The structure is the classic pyramid structure with a focus on culture and empowerment to achieve extraordinary employee motivation. Finally, Laloux introduces 'teal,' where self-management replaces the hierarchical pyramid. An organization is seen as a living entity with creative potential and an evolutionary purpose. While we will quickly diverge away from Laloux's thinking, his rainbow view of organizations is a prime example of a wonderful mental model. As you read the model, it is difficult not to try to map your own system into this category, and in turn, it will hopefully inspire you to wonder – or even feel provoked. The pitfall is to stay in the categorization mindset, though. Laloux's model is a sensemaking model, and companies often display behaviors through the model depending on the context. Extrapolating the model trying to predict future leadership is a fallacy.

Laloux has a straightforward way of determining at which stage an operation operates. He simply phrases it as *'the stage through which its leadership tends to look at the world. Consciously or unconsciously, leaders put in place organizational structures, practices and cultures that make sense to them, that corresponds to their way of dealing with the world.* **This means**

that an organization cannot evolve beyond its leadership's stage of development.'

The **bold** enhancement of the last sentence is mine. It is a significant sentence because it is not enough to simply sit back and wait and let natural evolution take its place. Eventhough Laloux debates that Teal organizations are the natural next step for us as humans, the resemblance to nature stops because evolution is not guaranteed.

As leaders, we pull organizations towards our state of consciousness, which goes both ways. This means that a leader can pull back an otherwise evolved organization from a later state, with inefficiencies to follow. At the same time, leaders can exert a strong pull forward by setting in place structures, practices, and cultures to help employees adapt to behaviors of more complex paradigms that they have not yet as individuals fully integrated.

This is a core part of managing complex systems – setting the proper enabling constraints. Teal organizations have often been described as leaderless, yet we claim that leadership is the cornerstone for change. Hence, we have already divulged one of the conclusions of leadership in the modern organization: Leadership is about enabling change. It's about enabling diversity. It is about creating an environment in which the organization thrives and evolves. It's about allowing it to happen. It might also be worth noticing that while leaders might not play such a significant role in teal organizations, it doesn't mean that leadership does not play

"

Teal organizations have often been described as leaderless, yet here we are claiming that leadership is the cornerstone for change

an important role. It absolutely does, but in a distributed way through empowerment. Before we use the word "empowerment," let's dive into power and empower as words and wonder what they mean.

Since the '70s (or thereabouts, the origin is unknown), *empowerment* has been a term gaining increasing popularity in leadership literature. However, the *power* we're addressing here is more closely related to philosophy than leadership. The French sociologist Pierre Bourdieu introduced Symbolic Power as a term for the unsaid yet influential power in any social structure. Because this power has never been addressed openly and specifically, it travels through different constructs. This unsaid, symbolic power exists all around us, especially in organizations. We're making the intangible tangible by giving it a name and talking about it. It is about putting words to the unsaid power structures and placing the power where it belongs.

Some different types of unspoken power:

Power by owning classifications or definitions. The person who owns the right to classify somebody or to define a class of persons has considerable and invisible power. There are unspoken expectations for various categories of people or processes. You are expected to behave in a certain way if you are a customer, a client, a citizen, an inmate, a patient, etc.

Example: The HR manager of an organization defines a new process to grow talents and handle problematic employees. She introduces two new definitions; "Talent" and "Evaluate Further." The purpose is that each manager can classify high-performance employees as talents and low performers as "evaluate further." It is evident that the manager has classification power, but less obvious that the HR manager has a lot of power by owning the definition of what the manager can classify. This power is not necessarily a bad thing, but it is also not necessarily a good thing. However, if a definition does not follow the classification, it can become counterproductive. Let us continue with the example of "talent." We all use the word from time to time, yet we probably have different interpretations of what it means.

Talent used to be a unit of measure and can be traced back at least 6000 years. Back then, before currencies, you might wear your wealth around your wrist or neck as precious metal chains. We still see this behavior today when people wear gold necklaces or bracelets. Back then, you could un-pick a chain of your bracelet – a talent – and use your talent to pay for goods or services. Talent literally means "sca-le" and comes from the ancient Greek τάλαντον (talanton). A talent was something you had that could be exchanged for goods and services. With the introduction of currencies and coins, the word talent stopped being a specific value and became a symbol. You could exchange talent for goods and services, but talent could also be a skill or aptitude. Today, sometimes talent means "this person is talented and can become something with a lot of training." Or talent could also mean "this person has years of practice, as a real ta-lent and can teach others to become excellent." Depending on who you talk to, talent can be a *potential* – a value that is not yet there, but we see all the right signals. Or a talent can be existing and evident – the value is clearly there. Both definitions are as right as they are wrong, yet we still see organizations classify people as talents without knowing if they agree with the definition.

Power by the ability to access symbolic violence. Bourdieu introduces something he calls "symbolic capital," – a ge-neric term for any species of capital that is perceived th-rough socially cultivated classificatory schemes (prestige, attention, titles, etc.). It is called symbolic violence if a per-son uses symbolic capital to dominate another individual.

It might be a patient who has developed a dependency on a nurse because the nurse has knowledge of the patient's disease, and the patient looks up to the nurse for guidance. The patient gives the nurse power because of the symbolic capital (knowledge). In this context, symbolic violence is often most visible when someone has been given the task of controlling real capital, which provides that person with huge symbolic capital. It might be a financial controller, a Project Management Office, or some other centralized place where departmental budgets and resources are distributed. In extreme cases, a change in a number in a spreadsheet can have real-life consequences for an employee somewhere else. The visible power of the leader versus the invisible power of the finance team is something to have on the radar. The visible power belongs to the manager who must let go of two employees due to resource constraints and budget savings, and the unspoken power belongs to the budget responsible.

Power by owning the governance principles. This is very close to what the French philosopher Michel Foucault calls Pastoral Power. The person who writes the guidelines that everyone must follow has power. Just look at the ten commandments and how much they have shaped the world. Secondly, the person who governs, that principles and guidelines are to be followed, has power. Here, Foucault compares the pastor who judges if the congregation has followed the religious guidelines. In this context, organizations of a specific size are likely to have governance structures and procedures. The people writing these guidelines and

It is imperative to limit the amount of invisible power in the organization

those assigned to assure compliance have received enough symbolic capital to have power. In modern organizations, governance is seen to take on two different paths. They are enabling constraints and governing constraints. Imagine a beetle. It does not have bones and a skeleton as we do. It has an exoskeleton, which shapes the beetle. It allows the beetle to grow, but it also limits its growth. It is a governing constraint.

In contrast, a human skeleton is an enabling constraint. A person can grow muscles, meat, or fat, supported by the skeleton. This is an enabling constraint. Per definition, power is needed to move or influence. The person who has power can move or influence. Thus, it is imperative to limit the amount of invisible power in the organization. The first step is to put words to the power. Giving the power a name becomes tangible and moves from being unsaid and invisible into something deliberate. This means that we can direct power to where it makes the most sense and not just a priori put it on the shoulders of leaders. Specifically, we can direct power to a group of people – a team.

This is the definition of an empowered team and leads us back to the opening statement:

Now that we know what power is, we also know how to control it. Specifically, we know how to transfer power and identify who has it. That is an essential property because many delegations are not real delegations. Often, they are, "please do my job for me." This is the case if the work is delegated without the power. You must name it to tame it – an appropriate phrase coined by Daniel Siegel.

Psychological Safety

Imagine a workplace where everyone speaks their mind, regardless of what others might think of them. A place where asking questions is not a sign of ignorance but a sign of a desire to learn. A place where it is safe to admit mistakes without being seen as incompetent but instead as someone willing to take a risk to learn new things. A place where you can freely propose new ideas without coming off as being intrusive.

The conditions for such a workplace are called psychological safety. Although the term found its way into organizational theory in the 1960s[19], it has especially gained influence in recent years due to Google's Project Aristotle and work done by Amy Edmondson[20]. In a psychologically unsafe environment, we often see a particular variation of *argumentum ad populum* called the Abilene Paradox[21]. This paradox is when a group of people decides on something that no one agrees with, but they believe the rest of the group does, so they comply with the group's thoughts. Or the cousin to the Abilene Paradox called "The Spiral of Silence," coined by Elisabeth Noelle-Neumann. The spiral of silence describes the phenomenon that people are more willing to express their opinion if they think it's popular. If they notice their opinion is unpopular with the group, they will be more inclined to be reserved and not speak up. Psychological studies, such as the Asch conformity Experiment, validates that this is a common behavior.

These behaviors typically happen when the team members fear the manager or, in some cases, alpha personalities in the team. A prime example of this is the Chornobyl disaster

in 1986 which could probably have been avoided had there been psychological safety. If you want an accessible introduction to that disaster, there's an excellent miniseries on HBO called "Chernobyl."

A common example is that the manager proposes something with an explicit prejudice toward the correct answer. If, in fact, this is not up for discussion, the team would be more satisfied with getting a direct order. If it, on the other hand, is up for debate, the manager should simply sit back and listen to the feedback from the team. A group with psychological safety would be comfortable saying out loud if they think differently from the manager.

Sometimes organizations like to measure the level of psychological safety, and if done correctly, that might work, but there are some traps.

Team A is in a psychologically safe environment. Team B is not. Which team makes the most mistakes?

When the results are in and show that team A makes the most mistakes, will that cause a knee-jerk reaction to say that psychological safety is terrible? Probably, until they realize that Team A is much more open about their mistakes and does not try to hide them, as Team B does, due to fear of repercussions.

There are many tools and processes out there to help foster and cultivate psychological safety. The above-referenced book by Amy Edmondson is a great example. But the truth is, it all comes down to the person(s) with any of the powers described in the previous chapter on Power.

If you are the boss and don't genuinely want your team to contradict you when they think you're wrong openly, you will never achieve psychological safety. If you are genuinely interested, then there is only one thing to do: demonstrate to the team that it is okay to speak up – again and again. It requires you to be brave and make it abundantly clear when something is not up for debate. If you try to hide it behind a rhetorical question, you will lose some of that hard-earned safety. Psychological safety enters the organization on a turtle but will leave on a hare. It is hard to earn but easy to lose.

The bakery

This chapter exemplifies some of the previous chapters through a bakery. Primarily because using an example from the digital world might be too close to home and might spawn too many biases. I must preemptively apologize to anyone who knows how to run a bakery because I haven't the slightest idea, and the examples I use might be entirely wide of the mark in the real world. This is not about the bakery, though. It's about the operating model. If you have followed all the chapters, you might be overwhelmed. How do you operate a digital team if you're used to working with requirement specifications and detailed delivery plans?

Meet Anna. She is the CEO of a small family-owned bakery on Shaw Street. "I run this bakery because I'm a skilled baker with a long accolade of prizes in my resume. We're placed at this address because there's a university nearby and several hotels and shops by the train station. This gives us a steady flow of potential customers, and we satisfy a market need by providing food in the morning for breakfast and lunchtime. The only other competitor in the food space is a pub that serves traditional 'pub food,' not as easy to grab on the go as our bread."

These are the ground conditions as to "the why" of the business. Unless these ground conditions change, this "why" is not revisited or revised. They don't run a yearly strategy session, but they do plan to act if any of the ground conditions change. Anna has read all the leadership books telling her to have a grand vision and a compelling "why" but has not found it necessary. It is not within the powers of her small bakery to "*end world hunger bun by bun,*" but they do have a small sign over the door saying: "*baked by us, loved by you.*"

Traditional companies run quarterly "Objective and Key Results" sessions, but Anna has bought into the kairos mindset and is running opportunity cycles as opportunities arise. In the current opportunity cycle, Anna has set up a strategic question. "Should we invest in the Hansson Farm, so we could be self-sufficient in wheat instead of buying it at market price?" Right now, there is an opportunity to buy the largest wheat-producing farm in the area. To figure out if this is a good idea, Anna puts up a hypothesis:

"Can we triple the amount of wheat used without cannibalizing on any of our other products"

For the investment to make sense, the shop would need to use three times as much wheat as they use today, and

Anna's team of skilled bakers is given this problem to solve. Notice how Anna is not bringing them a solution but a problem. A solution-based hypothesis reads, "Invent a new wheat-based product that customers will buy." This would instruct the team to spend time trying out new recipes and marketing activities, which may or may not give the desired outcome. The solution might not be a new product. It may not even be the bakers that solve it – it might be the marketing department trying to upsell their morning bread. The point is that Anna is delegating the solution to her teams by giving them this problem or opportunity.

The teams are working on their "response objective." A response objective is the team's saying, "Okay, boss, this is how we plan to help you." That is also how digital teams work with OKRs (Objective and Key Results). OKRs are not cascaded – they are a dialogue tool and a hierarchical way of distributing work and aligning teams.

The list of initiatives the teams will be working on varies. Some require different capabilities; some are more explorative in nature.

"Try out new recipes for cinnamon buns, targeting the students walking to and from the university."

"Invest in marketing activities and billboards at the nearby train station, measuring if we can have an increase of sales of existing products."

"Approach the pub and see if we can be their incumbent bread vendor for their dishes."

Some of these are good objectives, some are not so good, but the common trait is that these opportunities also live in kairos time. That is, there is no specific timeslot for innovation and product discovery. Instead of thinking about how long you should spend on discovery and innovation, think of it as how you can integrate the lessons learned into your main products.

Notice that this is not the only thing the teams are working on. The daily business continues, and they must bake and sell the daily bread. Not all work comes from objectives. There are streams of work that are just that, work, and where the OKR framework will not help. It is work where you know what to do (Bake roughly the same as yesterday). Here, there's no need for an explorative mindset. The explorative mindset answers a question such as "should we mill our own flour." The team knows that whole grain flour starts to degrade as soon as it is milled, as grain contains bran which oxidizes and begins to degrade when milled. How will the quality of the bread increase by insourcing milling, and is the quality increase enough for the market to recognize it and lead to higher income either through selling more, or a justifiable increase in price, following the increase in quality?

Anna's bakery is not divided into "thinkers" and "doers." The teams feel highly accountable for the bakery's success and understand the link between price, quality, market fit, etc.

Anna's bakery works in feedback loops. A loop is not specified in chronological time. There is no such thing as a two-week sprint. The length of the loop is defined in kairos. The value of the loop is measured in terms of outcomes and learning. The team understands that increase in knowledge is an increase in capacity. If the team learns how to optimize the rise in sourdough, decreasing the wait time for the dough to have a good rise, then that increases flow. Every new capability the team learns enables them to do more varied work, thus increasing flow. Anna understands that scaling the organization does not always equal hiring more full-time employees. It might also be achieved through learning and capability building, motivating the employees because they all love to learn new things.

Running in cycles instead of linear is a good idea. Running in kairos cycles is even better. Anna has read all the articles on 'agile burnout' that happens when teams continuously run in two weeks sprints. On Friday, they deliver their sprint commitment, and on Monday, they start a new one. Constantly sprinting can and will lead to employee burnout. When working in kairos, the team understands why it matters what they do and why it matters that they do it now. The team is involved in solving the company's strategic priorities, and they clearly see the link between their work and the current objectives at a company level.

Embracing the mindset of emergence and agency increases innovation. It removes the need for "an innovation team" because all employees are potential innovators. We do not know when, where, and how an opportunity emerges. Butter emerged when nomads discovered that the milk they carried in their sheepskin bags changed after a long day of riding. But the lightbulb didn't emerge from candlelight. It was invented with intention. Understanding the difference and working deliberately to give space to the agency is what makes an organization innovative.

You can run a bakery using these principles, but they are explicitly designed and deliberately for digital teams. One thing to remember is that you shouldn't just copy the principles outlined here. Understand the rules, then break them and make your own.

Summary – tl;dr

In 1955, Cyril Parkinson wrote an article in the Economist, beginning with "work expands to fill the time available for its completion." This quote has since become known as Parkinson's law and has primarily found its way into working with digital teams, and has been attributed to sources of waste. Whether that is true depends on how much governance and 'command-and-control' the organization exercises. However, with the introduction of kairos, the effect ceases to exist. In chapter one, we are wondering about time and how time has come to play such a significant role in our work and our plans. We discuss if there is an alternative to chronological plans and introduce one alternative – the ancient 'kairos.' Through examples, it is exemplified that not all deadlines can be in chronological time. When will you fall in love? How long does it take to catch a fish? When is the right time to publish this book? The more qualitative the question, the more it lends towards kairos.

Aristotle was fond of using kairos in his debates. He argues that when debating, there is a right time to come up with your arguments. If you come with them too soon, your opponent will have the opportunity to pick them apart, and you will run out of counterarguments. If you go with them too late, your opponent will have time to get the upper hand. When teaching, Aristotle would claim that the knack of knowing when to say what, is the ability to organize your speech in kairos.

After introducing kairos, we discuss agile ways of working at a conceptual level. We are not occupied with thoughts or opinions on the various agile methodologies. Other books have been written on that subject. The same goes for the frameworks that promise to scale agile. We propose that 'scaling agile' is an oxymoron. There is no such thing as scaling agile. Revisiting the definition of agile as a small cross-functional, empowered, and self-organizing team working in short feedback loops. This cannot be applied to a large team or an organization without breaking the meaning.

We conclude that you do not scale agile; you descale the work to fit an agile team.

With that in mind, we wonder how to organize the teams to support this model, and a suggestion is presented. This is followed by an anecdote about NUMMI – an American car factory trying to copy the Toyota ways of working, expecting similar results. The purpose of the chapter is to get the reader to wonder if there is always such a thing as "best practice" or if there are situations where "best practice" becomes "good practice."

The chapter is presented immediately after the chapter on the organization to ensure the reader pauses and wonders. To wonder if it makes sense to copy the suggestion directly or if changes can be made to make this fit the problem at hand even better. As the chapter concludes, the roads to success are all different.

The book takes a deep dive into a day of a software engineer. The presumption – or even assumption – is that there
are a lot of leaders out there, leading digital talents, that
have never actually been in the trenches, writing code that
real people will eventually use. Especially in big corporations, digital leaders come from various backgrounds and
often without solid software engineering experience. There
is nothing wrong with that. That just means the leader has
another profile and another set of capabilities. The hope is
that the chapters where we follow "Joe" will give such a
leader insight into how software engineers work and why
some actions, while well intended, can be counterproductive.
It is a rather technical chapter that introduces much of the
discourse used in a digital development team. A chapter on
metrics immediately follows it. A topic that has been debated
and misunderstood a lot. The chapter gives some concrete
examples through the eyes of the team, and the purpose
strays away a little bit from just 'make the reader wonder.'
It has been deliberately tightened somewhat to call for an
internal debate. Or, in Latin, "Pro Vocare" – to call forth a
voice. This is the etymology of provoking. So, if you, as the
reader, felt a bit provoked and wanted to disagree with the
chapter, that was entirely intentional.

If the book had served its purpose up to now, the reader
would leave the previous chapter slightly provoked and wondering. Now is the right time to talk about business apophenia. The blindness that executives seem to have when introduced to new ways of portraying the world. We discuss
how groupthink and identical backgrounds of today's leaders

hinder wondering. The book proposes that adding some diversity to the thinking of the group might be an excellent method to induce some wonder or provoke the status quo.

We then take a small break to introduce wicked problems. A wicked problem is a problem that doesn't have an answer. It can only become better or worse. Solving a Rubik's cube is not wicked. Even though there are millions and millions of positions for the cube, there is one single solution that will ensure the faces of the cube are all the same color. Climate change is a wicked problem – at least for now. We can all act and make it better or worse. We then wonder how we tackle wicked problems and conclude that the way most digital teams work today can probably be improved. Knowing the inner psychology of a digital team, we know that teams have a self-preservation mechanism, just as much as the people populating said team. This means that organizing in product teams can counter innovation. If the teams build windmills to fight global warming, they will probably never pivot to building nuclear reactors. That would be outside the teams' capabilities and, in turn, would mean that the skillset would need to be different. The team would, in effect, fire themselves. We wonder if this extreme example has merit in how digital teams work in product teams today. Taking a small step towards provoking, we propose a different way of thinking about digital teams. Creating small, stable, long-lived capability teams allows these capabilities to be in play wherever that capability is needed, aligning them to work streams or platforms. We propose that work flows to teams, instead of moving people to the teams with the most work.

The chapter on wicked problems was born from a need to talk about motivation. Still, when the chapter was done, there was more to be said about motivating digital teams, especially software engineers, so the book starts to wonder if they are motivated differently from or similar to others you might have been leading in the past. Drawing on the existing body of knowledge, we distinguish between extrinsic and intrinsic motivation. There's a difference between being motivated and being satisfied; we exemplify how a digital team feels. We wonder about the short idiom "work is work." Of course, work is work, but take a moment to wonder what that actually means. Work has been equivalented to what is on the backlog or to-do list for a digital team. Yet the teams have been asked to do a multitude of other things, not appearing on the list on which most of them are measured. It is that work that is meant by the first "work." Work not appearing on a to-do list is still work, and it is a big demotivator of teams building software. The reason for putting this so bluntly in writing is that it is hard to understand if you are not a software engineer by trade or craft. Hence, the hope is that you, as the leader of the digital teams, will listen – and listen carefully when the teams talk about what motivates them. While it might sound like a platitude at first, some real insights can be found. And motivated teams create better work.

While writing the chapter on motivation, and because of the focus on software engineers, it felt like the right place to talk about another big topic for digital teams: technical debt. Not just (but also) in the realm of motivation but also in terms of how to build software on a philosophical level. During the chapter, the path of wondering is again left for a while to call forth the reader's voice. Pro vocare. To provoke. A cornerstone of many a digital transformation is being challenged. The idea that software should only be written once. We wonder if that is actually a good strategy and if this will eventually slow down the flow of the teams, increase dependencies and slowly glue all the teams together in a big monolith. We conclude that "it depends."

After a provoking chapter, we return to being wonderful. Through a series of examples, we wonder about many of the world's great inventions and how they were not invented but rather emerged. At one point, researchers were developing a pill for high blood pressure using a chemical called Sildenafil. During the chemical trials, they wondered why the patients rarely returned the unused medications. This did not happen in other trials. This wondering led to the discovery of Viagra, as the patients found the drug had a side effect of which the scientist was not initially aware. Many inventions emerge, and we talk about how to make space for emergency. We discuss how agency should be considered an essential part of any organization working with innovation. We do not spend enough time wondering about the fact that agency is fragile and how the power of agency is exponential.

The wonder continues with a powerful chapter on power. Taking a philosophical view on the invisible power structures in any organization, the reader is encouraged to wonder if any of those constellations exist and if they can be made visible. We clearly describe the different types of invisible power that exist. The person who writes the rules has power, and so do those enforcing them. The persons providing the resources have power. The one with the knowledge has power. Many different types of power exist in organizations, and we make a point about naming them to tame them. We wonder if there is anything positive about having invisible power structures and conclude that reducing as many as possible is essential. We talk about empowerment and propose to bring decision power to the people who understand the problem instead of bringing the problem to the people with decision power.

Writing the chapter on power was difficult because it touches on many fundamental areas of organizations and their invisible balance of power. It makes you wonder who drives the school bus and makes the crucial decisions. When you think about it, in the context of your organization, people, groups, and committees immediately come to mind—people with invisible, unsaid power. Groups having power by owning classifications. Committees having power through governance. But even if you can identify them, do you speak up? This inspired a short chapter on psychological safety. It is short because it is not about why psychological safety is important. Many a good book has been written about that. The chapter is a gentle reminder that psychological safety is something you work for and earn. It enters on a turtle but can leave on a rabbit.

And the book ends with the example of a bakery trying to apply the thoughts presented throughout. As it turns out, as a conclusion, this doesn't quite cut it on its own.

So instead, the final chapter came to be.

A simple summary of all the wonders, thoughts, and ideas we explore together.

As you put this book down – I hope, wonder – do remember that you, the world you live in, and the people you inspire are all full of wonders.

Thank you for walking this path with me.

You are wonderful.

References

1   Lee, Bruce "Tao of Jeet Kune Do: New Expanded edition" (2011).

2   Human Relations 1951; 4; 3E. L. Trist and K. W. Bamforth. Technological Content of the Work System Defences of a Work Group in Relation to the Social Structure andof Coal-Getting.

3   Evans, Eric (2003). Domain Driven Design. Tackling complexity in the heart of software.

4   Womack, James P.; Jones, Daniel T. (2003), Lean Thinking: Banish Waste And Create Wealth In Your Corporation, Simon and Schuster.

5   Myers, Norman, and Jennifer Kent (1998), Perverse Subsidies.

6   Kim, Forsgren & Humble (2018). Accelerate: Building and Scaling High-Performing Technology Organizations

7   Conrad, Klaus (1958). Die beginnende Schizophrenie. Versuch einer Gestaltanalyse des Wahns Georg Thieme Verlag.

8   Taylor, Fredric (1911). The principles of scientific management.

9 Weick, K. E. (1995). Sensemaking in organizations. Thousand Oaks: Sage Publications.

10 Culture and point of view. Richard E. Nisbett, Takahiko Masuda. Proceedings of the National Academy of Sciences Sep 2003, 100 (19) 11163-11170; DOI: 10.1073/pnas.1934527100.

11 Ostrom, E. (2008). The Difference: How the Power of Diversity Creates Better Groups, Firms, Schools, and Societies. By Scott E. Page. Princeton: Princeton University Press, 2007.

12 Phillips KW, Liljenquist KA, Neale MA. Is the Pain Worth the Gain? The Advantages and Liabilities of Agreeing With Socially Distinct Newcomers. Personality and Social Psychology Bulletin. 2009; 35(3):336-350.

13 Thiel et al (2021). The paradoxical effect of employee monitoring on deviance. Journal of Management 1-32

14 Cagan, Marty (2008). Inspired. How to create tech products that customer slove.

15 Skelton, Pais et al (2019). Team Topologies. Organizing Business and Technology Teams for Fast Flow. IT revolution press.

16 Ryan & Deci (2000). Contemporary Educational Psychology. Volume 25, Issue 1, January 2000, Pages 54-67

17 Parsons, Kua & Ford (2017) Building Evoltionary Architecture.

18 Laloux, Frederic (2014): Reinventing Organizations

19 Knowles, Malcolm S. (January 1967). "PERSONAL AND ORGANIZATIONAL CHANGE THROUGH GROUP METHODS. By Edgar H. Schein and Warren G. Bennis. New York: John Wiley & Sons.

20 Harvey, Jerry B. (1988). The Abilene Paradox and Other Meditations on Management. Lexington, Mass: Lexington Books.

21 Edmondson, Amy (2018). The fearless organization. Wiley & Sons.

Printed in Great Britain
by Amazon

11101242R00084